PRAISE FOR
THE REPUTATION BOOK

"This book is refreshingly jargon free, and it has given me a new approach as to how to build on reputation and gain referral-based business."
Rolf Nielsen, Director, Nielsen Business Services

"If you adopt only 10% of this book's message, you will increase your shareholder value by 100%."
Robert Warner, Portfolio FD, The FD Centre

"If you want to build business though reputation and referrals, look no further: this book sets out the clear principles that you need to comply with, and gives you the tools you need to apply them to your organisation."
Colin Mills, Founder and Chairman, The FD Centre

"Every business is now affected by the empowered online world: this is a world where none can afford to leave the issue of reputation and referrals to chance. This book addresses this issue head on and gives enormous help to all who read it and apply the ideas."
Henry Hutchings, Founder and CEO, Clever Student Lets Ltd

"In the age of online choice and customer power, reputation and referrals are the bedrock of any business, including my own. This book addresses this subject in a straightforward, easy to understand and easy to action way: one I'd thoroughly recommend."
Harriet Filewood, MD, Scotts Castle Holidays Ltd

"This book seriously challenged me from the outset to think about taking quality time to consider how referable I and my business really are: I highly recommend this book."
Ian Shreeve, Market Development Director, Bell Fruit Group

"A great guide to measuring where you are in pursuit of building your business reputation and gathering referrals, clear and simple rules: I'd highly recommend this book."
Chris Black, Managing Director, Sound Leisure Limited

"If you are serious about your business reputation and its importance then this is a great read. A concise book with a no-nonsense approach it delivers some wonderful advice on steering your business towards a greater reputation and those all important customer referrals."
Andrew Ludlow, Managing Director, Network Resource Management Ltd

"Businesses are all about people, and employees are as important as customers, this book points you in the right direction and makes you remember to value your staff as well as your customers. Business is like a relay race, and if the last person in the race drops the baton then the race is lost. An excellent, well written, good humoured and informative business book. This definitely goes the extra inch and was a pleasure to read."
Claire Naylor, Customer Services Director, Regal Gaming and Leisure

"This book sets out clear and simple rules for building reputation and gathering referrals: I'd highly recommend this book."
James Croft, Group Strategy and Investment Director, Ei Group Plc

Published by
LID Publishing Ltd
The Record Hall, Studio 204,
16-16a Baldwins Gardens,
London EC1N 7RJ, UK

524 Broadway, 11th Floor, Suite 08-120,
New York, NY 10012, US

info@lidpublishing.com
www.lidpublishing.com

A member of:

www.businesspublishersroundtable.com

© Guy Arnold & Russell Wood, 2017
© LID Publishing Ltd, 2017
Reprinted 2017

Printed in Latvia by Jelgavas Tipogrāfija

ISBN: 978-1-911498-40-7

Cover and page design: Caroline Li
Illustrations: Sara Taheri

THE
REPUTATION
BOOK

**SUPERCHARGE YOUR REPUTATION
AND BOOST YOUR SALES AND REFERRALS**

GUY ARNOLD &
RUSSELL WOOD

LONDON NEW YORK BOGOTA
MADRID BARCELONA BUENOS AIRES
MEXICO CITY MONTERREY SAN FRANCISCO
SHANGHAI

FOR OTHER TITLES IN THE SERIES...

CONCISE ADVICE LAB

SMALL BOOKS: BIG IDEAS

CLEVER CONTENT, DYNAMIC IDEAS, PRACTICAL SOLUTIONS AND ENGAGING VISUALS – A CATALYST TO INSPIRE NEW WAYS OF THINKING AND PROBLEM-SOLVING IN A COMPLEX WORLD

conciseadvicelab.com

CONTENTS

INTRODUCTION

Thanks for buying this book.

You may already be pretty good at what you do, you may also already enjoy a good reputation and have received some great referrals, or you may be just starting out ... or somewhere in between. Whatever your situation, this book will help you.

> 'YOUR BRAND IS WHAT YOUR CUSTOMER SAYS ABOUT
> YOU WHEN YOU'RE NOT IN THE ROOM'
> - JEFF BEZOS, CEO AMAZON

This small book offers a simple, systematic approach to reputation and referrals that is well proven and backed up by real situations and examples. You can use this in whatever way suits you best: we'd recommend skimming through it first, then looking at the key areas where you need to focus most.

But don't stop there.

Remember: **it takes a lifetime to create a reputation and a second to destroy one.**

Go back again and again, share this with friends and colleagues and keep working on everything you do in small methodical steps.

A journey of 1,000 miles starts with the first step.

This book is aimed at helping you do all the right things to build your reputation, continually and consistently, and then, through this, to systematically build referrals.

Remember: **you cannot truly get referrals until you consistently act in a 'referable' manner**, be it your organization, team or yourself – this is a fundamental principle that you cannot break. That's why it's about 'reputation and referrals' and not just 'referrals': **referrals follow reputation, not the other way around.**

THE DEFINITION OF 'REPUTATION & REFERRALS' (R&R)

Reputation: Customers come to us passively because of our reputation in the market.
Referrals: Customers actively refer other customers to come to us.
This book supercharges both!

So, we'll teach you systems to build your reputation first, and then to systemise your referrals to help you create a constant and consistent stream of them.

You can use this book as:

- A full guide
- A pocket reference
- Or just to give you continual hints and tip to keep you on track and use as a reminder

We hope it adds real value to you.

TAKE ACTION:
GO THE EXTRA INCH!

Ok, so you've bought business books before, and you've been on training courses, and, despite all the hype, the impact has been less than spectacular, right?

Well, you're not the only one. Most business books, systems and training courses massively over promise and under deliver. So, here are our suggestions:

1. The material in this book is dynamite: but dynamite needs to be handled carefully and properly in order to ignite!

2. Take it slowly and aim to have one small victory every week: we call this **'Go the Extra Inch'**: if you focus on planning and executing one small step every week, after a month, you'll have

taken four steps forward (more than after most training and development), and after a year you'll have over 50 steps! That will make a huge difference.

So, for every point in the book, we've included an exercise that can be worked on in a week. All you have to do is choose your inch each week, keep referring back to this little book, and go for it. (We call these 'Thinkabouts'.)

It's That Simple.

Your weekly **Action Plan**:

1. Choose a 15-minute slot in your week and stick to it (Friday after 5pm or Sunday evenings seem to work best for most people).

2. Review the inch you committed to last week, and pat yourself on the back for any progress you made.

3. Review your situation: what needs addressing next?

4. Every week, choose an inch from this book and plan to action it: then schedule this into your calendar as a crucial action/appointment for the week.

5. Consider accountability: what measure will you use to determine the success of this inch?

6. Share this with someone (maybe a coach, friend or co-worker), to ensure you are held accountable.

7. Do it (don't let anyone steal your inch!)

8. Congratulate yourself and review in your next 15 minute weekly slot.

Success is that simple. All you need to do is to put the 15 minutes aside in your calendar and do it.

PART ONE

BACKGROUND AND SOCIAL REVOLUTION

BACKGROUND

History moves slowly, and it's usually not until you're out the other side that historians will look back wisely and say: "That was a time of this or that massive change."

For hundreds of years, we have lived in the 'Industrial Age': let's look at the four primary mindsets that are associated with the Industrial Age:

1. **One-Way Mass Communication** (after the invention of the printing press)

2. **Domination of Big Businesses and Brands**

3. **Win-Lose Sales Mindset** (sales processes focused on winning new business often at the expense of customer loyalty)

4. **Command and Control**

The Industrial Age was **sales and marketing focused**. Everything was designed around getting sales and profits (almost at the expense of anything else). **This approach worked because customers had limited access to third-party reviews, information and alternatives.**

What's happened is that we are now moving from that one-way communication mindset of the Industrial Age, into a business world of two-way communication. This two-way communication is known as the **'social revolution'**.

This is generating a **massive** change in human (and especially customer) behaviour: and most organizations are blissfully unaware of the size of the change.

In order to build reputation and referrals in this new age you have to be fantastic at delivering consistent service and continually improving the customer experience (reputation) and leveraging this to drive repeat business, cross sales and new customers (referrals), rather than traditional sales and marketing.

But, as stated, many organizations, individuals and brands haven't recognised this change yet and, if they have, they are often too set in their old ways to do anything about it. So, they may be staggering and failing to adapt effectively to this new world of the social revolution where:

- ✓ There is a two-way communication
- ✓ No one believes the marketing bullshit that used to be effective any more
- ✓ There is Global choice and transparency
- ✓ Customers are engaged, informed and motivated for something better
- ✓ Customers can review any organization or product in an instant
- ✓ Prospective customers believe other customers' opinions above all else

Here are two questions that we are going to answer. By the time you finish this book, you will be able to answer these two questions for your organization, and take the necessary actions to make them happen, continually and consistently.

1. If the world is changing, then what can we do in our organization to take advantage of that change?

2. How can we properly use the power of the customer to help us build our organization through reputation and referrals?

Back to recent history: this two-way communication in the market has also brought a blight with it. That blight is that the market is overly saturated with information. The more this world of communication grows, the less REAL communication people are getting.

So, **in order to break through that mess and become someone who stands out in a crowd, you have to be special. You can't just be satisfactory anymore. You have to be great or remarkable** – otherwise you're almost invisible!

You might have a website and that website might be perfectly optimized (that's satisfactory). But most websites are still based on the one-way communication philosophy, and your target customers are frankly too busy, have too much info, and can't find you.

Don't take this the wrong way. There's nothing wrong with having a website. But a website on its own is rarely a route to anything hugely valuable in this socially engaged, two-way mass communication world. It's usually just a new take on old marketing ideas.

In order to build a reputation in this brave new world, you need to be **remarkable** and in order to get referrals you need to be **referable**.

These are generally different aspects of the same thing, and in this book, we start with being remarkable (so you build your reputation) and then tell you how to put systems and processes in place to turn this consistent remarkability into continual streams of referrals. First one then the other: what we call **'blindingly obvious common sense'**.

For example, almost every new organization giant you can name, and almost every long-term success story knows this principle and applies it rigorously.

New organizations giants: Amazon, Google, Facebook, Uber, Airbnb (and the list will continue to grow).

Long-term success stories: John Lewis, Richer Sounds, Barbour, BMW, Apple.

All of them without exception applied this principle, they've grown through remarkability and referability, **not** through sales and marketing.

THINKABOUT 1 - DO SOME RESEARCH

- What organizations are you fiercely loyal to and why?
- What organizations do particularly well or badly in your marketplace?
- What do your customers think (hint: call them and ask them)?
- If you could wave a magic wand and make your organization highly remarkable and referable, what main things would you change today?

THERE IS NO SUCH THING AS AN UNIMPORTANT CUSTOMER

This social revolution presents both a massive threat and opportunity for every organization. Admittedly some markets are more sensitive to this than others, but this now affects ALL markets and is becoming more powerful every day. This is an issue that no organization can afford to ignore.

- The **threat** is, of course, that any less than satisfactory customer experience can spread around the globe at the touch of a button and the speed of light
- And, conversely, the **opportunity** is that remarkable and referable experiences can spread just as fast

'Traditional' marketing simply cannot compete!

While this new customer power has resulted in the quick spreading of great reputations, and thus the explosive growth of new great organizations – to the point that almost every day in the news we hear of 'another one' and the 'next big thing' – human nature dictates that mud sticks and people love to spread bad news.

So, it's **more of a threat than an opportunity**, even though it's a massive opportunity.

Consider the case of 'United Breaks Guitars'. There's a long story behind this, but, in a nutshell, the guitar of a United Airlines' customer, Dave Carroll, was broken during a flight. After a long battle, they refused to offer any compensation, so instead Dave recorded a (very good) video about the incident on YouTube. This went viral, resulting in massive PR (and consequently share price) damage over many months. All from the bad experience of just one customer!

While most organizations will rarely experience the kind of nightmare suffered by United Airlines, **the real risk is that 'less than great' reputations continually spread**, sometimes even without the organization even being aware of it at all. **This results in business becoming significantly harder for the organization.** It may even drag them down, make marketing and selling a hugely tough exercise and force them to cost cut and offer deals that would be totally unnecessary if they were significantly more remarkable and referable.

It slowly and surely either kills or makes you.

A good example of this dichotomy is the success of Richer Sounds in the UK. Richer Sounds is famous for being remarkable (and is a Guinness World Record holder for sales per retail square foot), in the same market that saw the demise of a much larger and more heavily marketed rival, Comet, who were famous for being distinctly unremarkable.

THINKABOUT 2 - DO SOME RESEARCH

- Research Richer Sounds on the web: what do they do so well?
- Research 'United Breaks Guitars' on YouTube and the subsequent story of what happened

THE NEED FOR SOCIAL PROOF (OR, IN OLD TERMS, 'GREAT REPUTATION')

In this world of two-way communication, your organization must have social proof. People have to be talking about it. **So, your goal should be to maximize that social proof through genuine greatness** (and never through clever IT systems). This is going to become more and more important as systems continue to empower the customer and make it easy for future customers to find out what people really think about you (and your competition) – usually without you having any idea that they may be interested in you.

For example, an organization where social proof is obviously hugely important is a hotel. No one looks at a hotel's website; they focus on online reviews. You could argue that the only valid reasons for a hotel to have a website are to provide you with a phone number and a map of how to find them!

A website is often only a business card in today's world. It serves to provide information to consumers, but it's rarely a great marketing tool (unless it's a specific shop front in itself) – your PR and marketing is now in the hands of social proof, customer reviews and general reputation.

- Is social proof, always right? No!
- Is social proof equally as important for all types of organization? No!

But it is where the market is going and in time it will become business critical for every market. And, of course, if you want the best grass and the most notice, you need to get there before the herd.

A good example of this change hitting and changing specific business sectors occurred recently in real estate. A traditional market that has been sedentary for a long time has now been turned on its head by cost effective and very high quality online competition. It's happening everywhere, to everything; don't get caught with your pants down!

So, what do you need to do? Luckily the answer will become clear as we go on and there's no need for panic.

THINKABOUT 3 - DO SOME RESEARCH

- Research your job role/market on Google News: what 'cutting edge' stories are beginning to emerge (what is 'interesting news' today is 'normal' tomorrow)
- Look at online freelancing sites: is there competition you were unaware of?
- Search 'The best [your role] in the world' and see what type of information you find
- Repeat monthly

THE MATHS:
WHY INVESTING IN REPUTATION AND REFERRALS IS WAY MORE PROFITABLE THAN 'TRADITIONAL MARKETING'

OK, so if this is all so blindingly obvious, then why do we have to read books about it, and why is great practice in this area as rare as hen's teeth?

Here's a list of issues that cause the problems:

The 'industrial age mindset': this has powered much of the industrial world and worked fine before the advent of two-way mass communication. This mindset resulted in 'command and control' systems in organizations, which, in turn, stops empowerment and feedback and means those making the vital decisions have no idea what's really going on and are not nearly nimble enough to respond change as needed. Despite being fatal to an organization, this mindset is still very common (as most Western-style education and upbringing still runs with these rules).

The 'animal instinct': the basic needs of all animals are to survive and procreate. This is driven by an ancient part of the brain called the amygdala. This part of the brain assesses everything that comes our way and then judges whether it's a potential threat or not. If it is, then it automatically triggers the 'fight or flight' response. The area of reputation and feedback is highly threatening to the amygdala, and can trigger it easily and continually. A 'fight or flight' response will not be great at helping us become referable. We need to learn how to calm the amygdala and respond effectively and constructively – more on this later.

The 'bottom line obsession': organizations are there to make money, period. Even 'not for profits' and charities have to make enough money to keep going (and flourish), so the act of 'making money' is very important! The problem comes when businesses stop aiming to be 'great' first and make money second (as a result of doing things properly), and instead aim to make money first – almost at any cost (and not worry that much about being 'great' any more). They then support the 'fake greatness' through clever PR, marketing and sales tactics. This shows up as:

(a) Focusing on the short term at the expense of the long
(b) Doing the profitable things at the expense of doing the 'right' things
(c) Sales driven by offers – at the expense of remarkability
(d) Shareholders at the expense of customers

And this mindset is **very** endemic even now in almost all organizations. This is one of the main reasons why it's so hard for such organizations to change and instead do the 'right' things consistently, in the belief that if they genuinely focus all resources on being truly remarkable and referable first, and then the profits will follow (not the other way round).

This is a revolutionary mindset (in all senses), and trying to change the 'normal way of doing things' and turning it on its head is neither easy nor quick.

So, what's the answer?

As we will see, the answer lies in beliefs, systems, behaviours and measures that overcome the Industrial Age Mindset, calm the amygdala and overturn the Bottom Line Obsession, and instead focus on **the one thing** above all else ...

... in good times and bad
... no matter if anyone's watching or not

Our purpose is to be remarkable and referable in all we do. If we do this consistently and keep improving, we will then be rewarded by customer loyalty, reputation, cross sales and referrals – and our costs of achieving this will be consistently low. **Then, and only then will we achieve long-term financial success – not the other way around.**

An example that proves this point is Amazon.com: 'Our vision is to be the Earth's most customer-centric organization.'

And if blindingly obvious common sense isn't enough and you're someone who only makes decisions on hard figures, have a look at this page of stats we've gathered from working in this field over the last 20 years. The evidence to support these ideas is all around us, we just need to have the vision and courage to accept it and change **properly** for the best long term success of everyone.

80% of 'satisfied' customers will use a different supplier next time – invest in loyalty

It is at least six times as expensive to get a new customer as it is to get an existing customer to return – invest in loyalty

96% of unhappy customers won't tell the organisation about it: they'll tell their friends instead – invest in feedback

News of bad customer experiences travels three times as fast as good news, and reaches at least 10 times as many people – invest in feedback

68% of customer defections are because of 'perceived indifference' – invest in loyalty and relationships

Most customer feedback systems ask the wrong questions in the wrong way and have return rates of < 15%, so most customers typically feel disengaged and unloyal – invest in feedback and loyalty

Prospective customers are at least three times as likely to believe independent reviews as the Organisation's own marketing – invest in feedback and loyalty

THINKABOUT 4 - DO SOME MATHS

- Take one of the ideas from the previous lists each week and run your stats through them ... the bottom line impacts will make your eyes water

WHY THIS MATTERS MORE THAN ANYTHING NOW

This is a very short section because you already know the answer:

- ✓ There is easy two-way global communication
- ✓ No one believes your marketing
- ✓ There is global choice and transparency
- ✓ Customers are engaged, informed and motivated for something better
- ✓ Customers can review any organization or product in an instant at the touch of a button
- ✓ Prospective customers believe other customers' opinions above all else
- ✓ There's nowhere to hide, no matter how much you spend on PR
- ✓ What do you need to have in order to fix this?

Simply put, **beliefs, strategies, processes, behaviours and measures systematically drive this cycle in a positive way.** This ensures that customers rave about you and refer you continually and stops you turning this into a negative cycle.

An enjoyable example of getting it wrong (and there are many to choose from every day):

> **A poster encouraging Sainsbury's workers to get customers to spend more was put up in a store window in error.**

The sign, urging staff to get people to spend an extra 50p, appeared in Stratford, east London. A customer took a picture and posted it on Twitter saying: ".@sainsburys not sure this is supposed to be in your window."

Sainbury's tweeted back to say it was meant for staff only, and asked the customer to reveal which store it was in. This then resulted in a highly amusing twitter conversation, in which the Sainsbury's representative became ever more frantic, which then went viral, resulting in over 4 million negative PR views of Sainsbury's in just a few days.

There is also a mirror story to this: the story was beautifully taken advantage of by a competitor retailer: within 24 hours Lidl had copycat posters up in their stores stating 'Let's encourage every one of our lovely customers to save as many 50ps as possible'. Brilliant (and, of course, it also went viral).

THINKABOUT 5 - GET YOUR BELIEFS RIGHT

- Every chain is only as good as its weakest link: are you doing what you do because you can make money without having to work too hard – or are you happy and confident that what you do is worthwhile work and makes a positive difference? Your choice, but remember: over time, your beliefs will become transparent to those around you

THE HUMAN NEED
FOR ATTENTION

Customers are emotional and unpredictable.

Customers have different physical needs, but similar emotional ones.

Customers want you to care about them and pay attention to them and be trustworthy in all you do. Then they will love you and help you succeed.

Customers will remember how they felt emotionally about your product or services, long after they have forgotten what those products or services were. These are called **'moments of truth'**.

If you connect with a customer emotionally, they will be loyal to you and will promote your products and services to their friends and colleagues.

If you abuse their emotions, they will do all in their power to harm you – if they don't get positive attention, they have an unfulfilled hunger, which they will go elsewhere to sate.

Consider small children; the key thing they want from their parents is attention. In fact, 'attention' is now being researched, because it may be that it is as much of a physical need for us as a species as sustenance. The only difference being that we won't physically die if we don't get it, but we do suffer emotionally.

Consider this:

- Research on orphans in developing countries (who had little or no attention in early childhood) show them to be physically incapable of loving others
- Research into life threatening diseases or major operations show a massive increase in recovery rates depending on the support and relationship situation of the patient

This is a subject not yet well researched, but the key learning principle is that if you genuinely give customers attention throughout their customer journey, they will repay you with world class levels of loyalty and reputation (and referrals). If you fail to do this and the best you can hope for is indifference and lack of loyalty.

Examples:

- Getting it right: Zappo's world conquering levels of customer loyalty and retention, driven by their obsessive and unswerving levels of customer attention – while retaining shoes
- Getting it wrong: Ratners jewellers in the UK went from being the largest jewellery chain in the UK to bankrupt in a very short time following widely reported negative comments on the quality of their products

THINKABOUT 6 - MORE RESEARCH

- Research getting this right and wrong (have a look at the story of Zappos and Ratners)
- View some videos of Tony Hseih of Zappos on YouTube explaining his philosophy of 'delivering happiness'

PART TWO

REPUTATION
AND
REFERRALS

SOCIAL REVOLUTION

In the pre-'social revolution' (SR) world traditional marketing was all about un-personalised mailing lists and being bombarded with irrelevant offers.

Referral marketing followed in the same vein: through bribes and offers. It was a huge, costly effort perpetuated by self-serving marketers, justifying their existence with the same old activity – all deemed necessary but expensive.

Even if their offer was outstanding, and the customer liked it, they probably wouldn't refer it to other people because you cannot buy people's integrity nor can you buy their engagement.

Even now, how many times do you click on the unsubscribe link because the after-sales is not relevant or personalised to you, or your data has been sold to a third party?

So, if after-sales marketing results are poor, marketers have to put even more focus on winning new customers. Marketing thus often remains focused on gaining new customers, rather than truly building R&R. It's traditional but highly ineffective in the SR world.

A couple of questions to reflect on:
Q: Who else is trying to get new customers?
A: Everyone, but it's not effective to compete with everyone else.

Q: Who already has a relationship with you, got past everyone else to deal with you, and is now being abused or forgotten?
A: A large number if you are in pre-SR traditional marketing mode. If you do this, YOU are making life much harder than it needs to be for YOURself

"Don't go where the herd has gone because all of the grass has been eaten" (Bob Dylan)

TWO KEY RULES

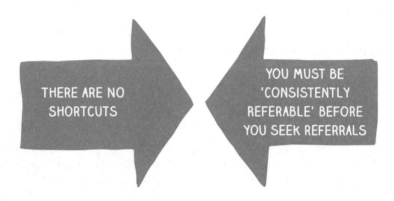

THERE ARE NO
SHORTCUTS

YOU MUST BE
'CONSISTENTLY
REFERABLE' BEFORE
YOU SEEK REFERRALS

The order and process: no short cuts!

One of the biggest steps is self-belief followed by a structured systemised process: here are the building blocks:

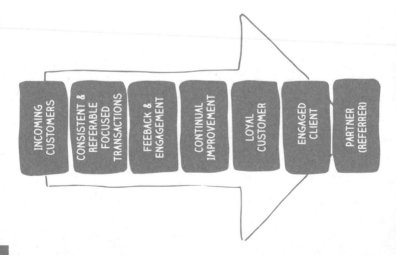

INCOMING CUSTOMERS

CONSISTENT & REFERABLE FOCUSED TRANSACTIONS

FEEBACK & ENGAGEMENT

CONTINUAL IMPROVEMENT

LOYAL CUSTOMER

ENGAGED CLIENT

PARTNER (REFERRER)

Poor organizations stop investing time and effort after they make a transaction.

Great organizations work holistically on every building block, all of the time.

BUILDING BLOCKS - WHO'S WHO?

INCOMING CUSTOMER – one who wants to learn about your products, services and people and how you engage as an organization.

LOYAL CUSTOMER – one who understands the value of what you offer, re-engages and understands your reputation but may seek an alternative provider.

ENGAGED CLIENT – one who accepts the value of your product or service, believes in your reputation, and only uses you.

PARTNER – one who wholly believes in your organisation and is enthusiastic to promote and refer you to others without question.

There's absolutely no substitute for continuous effort in your R&R activity based on your strategy, systems and actions. That all might feel like a relentless quest; it is – there's no shortcuts.

Example: in the pre-SR world, I worked in the leisure sector. I ran nightclubs for a major national operator. Our reputation was everything in order to build and maintain business. Referrals were critical. It took a year of relentless promoting, reflection, review, and building knowledge.

Years later I found out that the managing director had wanted to move me after a few months after I had started in my role due to an initial lack of growth, but was prevented from doing so by my immediate manager. He had become a partner in our mission, who importantly gave us the time to succeed. We became the Club of the Year (and had we been in the SR era we could have got there quicker and cheaper!).

It takes time to build R&R but you should always have the endgame in mind, and always work on it.

TAKE A LEAP OF FAITH - TALK TO PEOPLE; GET PEOPLE TO TALK

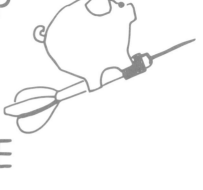

It's vital to get a few people to talk to a lot of people. Essentially, if you minimize the investment in delivery and after-sales, then you're headed into trouble. The problem is there's often not enough budget to spend on those two areas. Here's what I encourage you to do.

The key is to take money away from your marketing budget and put it into after-sales marketing.

It is important to remember that you have to **FUEL** your after-sales marketing activity to constantly drive the Reputation and Referral engine, **FUEL is**:

- **F**EEDBACK
- **U**NDERPINS
- **E**NGAGEMENT
- **L**OYALTY

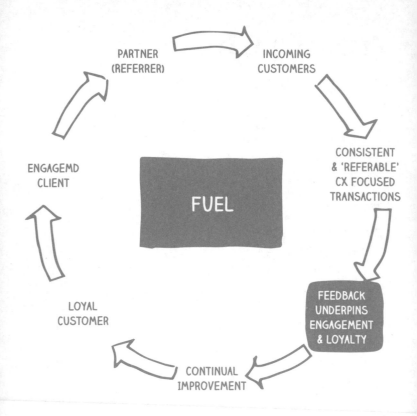

If you are not **FUEL**ling after-sales then there's no way for you to know the relationship you have with your customers. They might be loyal or they might be unfaithful; there's really no way to know unless you are making an effort.

FUELling demands that you commit energy and planning to obtain the feedback necessary to drive R&R. Create some uninterrupted time with your customers, both internal and external. Set up one-to-one or group sessions to review your feedback. Then prioritise and allocate your next actions. Then repeat the process.

Face-to-face, FaceTime, Skype or by telephone are more personal methods of **FUEL**ling feedback.

By choosing different Internal Customers to seek and review feedback you will also grow the skill base and confidence within your organization.

This investment in after-sales marketing builds customers, sales, order size, margins and profit and allows innovation to thrive. It also reduces costs, mistakes, customer attrition, aggravation and dissatisfaction.

It's well worth doing!

And it cannot be left to chance: it must be deliberate and systemised.

The problems with not having a system include:

- No focus
- No clarity or alignment which leads to confusion
- Employees and customers are more difficult than they need to be
- Fear and self-doubt – "Am I doing the right thing?"
- Fear of action leads to inaction, which in turn cannot build your reputation, paralysis sets in

REPUTATION ALWAYS STARTS OFF SHAKY

In this SR world, your reputation always starts off shaky. Bad news travels as fast as you can tweet. You could get a hundred things right and one thing wrong but that one bad thing is going to be the focal point of the conversation, and that conversation will be online and out of your control.

However, every sword has two edges. Now, in the SR era, this is a great time to obsessively focus on your reputation because if you get everything right then your customers will spread it for free.

There is some good news here. We have found through research that as online reviews and social media become more accessible, **the likelihood of people sharing good news is becoming more significant.**

During the Industrial Age, it was more difficult for consumers to communicate with each other so they only bothered to communicate when there was a serious issue. As it becomes easier to communicate, they are sharing good things more often. **That's really good news for people and organizations who genuinely work on getting it right.**

REPUTATION IS NOT LIMITED TO YOUR 'PAYING' CUSTOMERS

Your Internal Customers (employees) play a huge role in your Reputation. They are truly In Charge, every minute of every day. Others who play a key role in your reputation are:

- 'Lapsed Customers'
- 'Not Yet Customers'
- Your Suppliers
- Your Community

Command and Control versus Empowerment

During the Industrial Age of one-way communication, everything was based on the process of command and control.

The philosophy was:

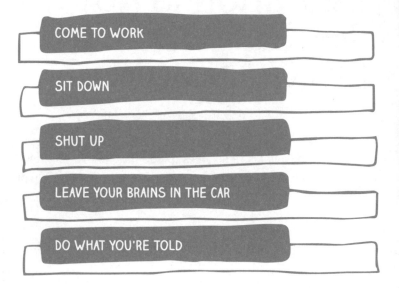

COME TO WORK

SIT DOWN

SHUT UP

LEAVE YOUR BRAINS IN THE CAR

DO WHAT YOU'RE TOLD

Many organizations still operate under this philosophy, even though it's just not effective anymore. I'm sure that you have had a job that fell under the command and control category. If so, did you even remotely enjoy **going** to work or did you dread it? Did you know that customers can pick up on the vibe generated from a poor work environment?

With that said, command and control simply doesn't work anymore. In today's world, the effective philosophy is:

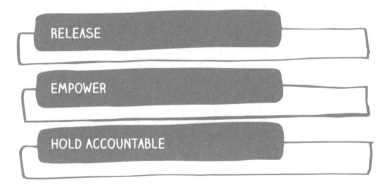

RELEASE

EMPOWER

HOLD ACCOUNTABLE

With the competition that exists in today's world, if you do not follow these principles, you're just not going to be fit for purpose in your field. You have to ensure that your employees are working to their optimum ability, in a culture and working environment that promotes **great** R&R.

A WORD OF WARNING - BEWARE OF QUICK FIXERS!

It can be dog eat dog out there! You can be certain that there are people who will prey on your organization's vulnerability when you're struggling. They are known as 'quick fixers' and there are a lot of them out there.

Here are a couple of easy signs to spot them:

- "We can get your social media marketing working"
- "We can get you 2,000 Facebook likes"

If you are approached by someone who offers to fix something in your organization, always ask yourself one important question:

How many customers will it actually bring into your organization?

Most of these instant claim marketers will avoid the question. They are interested in providing simple things that you're paying them for – numbers. **Quick fixes don't work!**

'TRYING TO BE NICE' IS NOT THE SAME AS 'BEING CONSISTENTLY REFERABLE.'

The word 'nice' has no substance. It is a word with no gravitas and customers can easily see through fake 'niceness'. So trying to **pretend** to be nice is going to come back and bite you because it has no depth of meaning and customers **hate** fakery.

By falsely pretending to be nice you are:

- Not truly valuing your customers
- Not empowering your employees
- Not focusing on your R&R above all else

This often leads to creating havoc!

There is no quick fix. That's why your organization needs to focus so much on the inside-out approach, as well as systemising this for consistency.

You Have to be Consistently Referable Before You Can Ask For Referrals.

Example: We were leaving to go on holiday one Saturday. The car key fob would not lock the car and we needed to park it safely for a week in a public car park. We went to the nearby local dealership and explained our dilemma. Here was the reaction without any consideration: "Sorry! We cannot do that for you, the mechanic has two jobs to do. We can book you in for Monday." Their next nearest dealership was eight miles away. We rang them. Here was the immediate response: "If you can get here in the next hour we can do that for you."

If only they had a consistent approach and a simple system of R&R in all their dealerships!

BE A BEAR!
THE FOUR PRINCIPLES
OF HUMAN BEHAVIOUR

We all like to think we are unique, even special in some way! In this world of celebrity culture and instant social media fame or notoriety, we can be noticed instantly, and for better or for worse we are wedded to the web.

Irrespective of our own skills, personality and appearance every human being has four universal behavioural traits.

You can rely on them as the bedrock for building your reputation, since knowing how customers and employees naturally react and respond provides the key ground rules on to how you build reputation and gain referrals.

People always act like **BEARs**

Belief; **E**motion; **A**ctions; **R**esult(s) = **BEAR**s

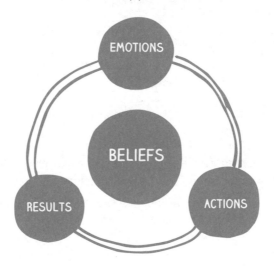

1. BELIEFS

Every one of us is unique, and we have our own unique beliefs. No two people have the exact same set of beliefs. It's important to appreciate that your **I**nternal **C**ustomers are working with you at the moment because of those beliefs.

Some people go to work with the single belief, that is "I need money".

How good would that one belief be in a global, hyper-competitive market? Alone, it wouldn't be worth a lot. If it's **just** about money, then you're really in trouble because you will never get the effort and genuine commitment that you need to compete in today's world.

On the other hand, beliefs like, "I believe in this organization's purpose" or "I love what we do" are going to be worth a lot more. Most people put a lot more than their monetary needs into the decision of choosing a job.

You have to know the beliefs of your **I**nternal **C**ustomers so that you can engage with them on a very deep level. In return, you also have to share your own beliefs with them. Be very clear about your beliefs as an organization.

They must be genuine and worthwhile to get the level of commitment you'll need in the SR world.

CUSTOMER FOCUSED MISSION

Try putting those beliefs in writing. You only need **one** short powerful sentence using simple words. It will help you to crystallise and consolidate your beliefs. We call that "The Customer Focused Mission".

Get a group of co-workers (and customers) together and give it a go!

Think about a pub. The people who work in a pub have to like 'looking after people' and 'helping people to have fun'. It has to be more than just coming to work and getting paid. If you own a pub, it's essential that you hire people who love interacting with others.

You can teach them everything else but you cannot teach some-one what to believe or how to behave.

Your mission might be something like, 'for everyone to leave with a smile and keen to return.'

Or a professional services organization may even have referrals as part of its mission, 'to do what we do well, so that every customer would want to refer us.'

This 'Customer Focused Mission' would then form the basis of every strategy, process and measure in your organization, and it will align behaviours and attract like-minded people (if you stick to it). This will make recruitment and management much easier.

Note: This is not the clichéd, traditional mission statement devised by the board on an away day in a five-star hotel (with a spa)!

2. EMOTIONS
Beliefs are the driving force behind emotions.

So, the next step is to figure out what emotions are behind the beliefs of your customers (internal and external). Only when you know what their emotions are, can you attempt to engage these customers effectively. Here are the questions that you must address – honestly:

- How are you engaging on an emotional level?
- Do you genuinely care about customers or are they just a number?
- Do your customers believe that you are genuinely trying to get it right or do they think you're just in it for the money?
- Do you go out of your way to make their lives easier?
- Are you genuinely trustworthy?
- And most important of all – **Do you really value the customer or is this just lip service?**

Being competent at your daily tasks is one thing – most business owners are very competent on a skill level – but competence isn't enough to thrive in today's market.

You have to genuinely care about the emotions of both internal and external customers

Remember that we are taking an inside-out approach so it all starts with your **I**nternal **C**ustomer.

3. ACTIONS

You can learn everything that you need to do but that knowledge is useless if you don't take action.

Knowledge without action is **delusion** and, action without knowledge is foolhardiness.

Once you know the emotional driving force behind your customers then you need to take action to make the most of it.

THINKABOUT 7 - ACTIONS

- What sort of actions do you take on a daily basis?
- Are they small, continual and attainable?
- Are they focused on consistency and continual improvement?
- Are you continually gathering feedback?
- Do you systematically take action on all feedback?
- Do you work with your team to help them to become continually more empowered?
- Do you systematically meet with your Internal Customers to improve and grow in themselves?
- Are all your actions aligned with your 'Customer Focused Mission'?
- Do you use your customers' REAL needs as a constant filter?

4. RESULTS - WHAT GETS MEASURED GETS DONE

If you can measure something then you can improve it. Unfortunately, many customer service measurements have a negative effect because:

- They ask too many questions
- They are the wrong questions
- They have no meaningful score
- They are not regular
- They provide little helpful feedback

And worryingly they just look for **satisfaction**!

What you really want to know from your customers is:

- Have we achieved our CFM?
- Why?
- What else could we do to improve your experience?

LEAD V. LAG MEASURES

Focusing on measuring your processes, behaviour and your reputation are **lead** measures. They enable you to influence the future. This type of measure relies on a release, empower, hold accountable culture.

Looking periodically at quantitative numbers are **lag** measures. **Lag** measures are those that have already happened, it's history and you cannot influence history. This type of measure is prevalent in the 'command and control' way of working.

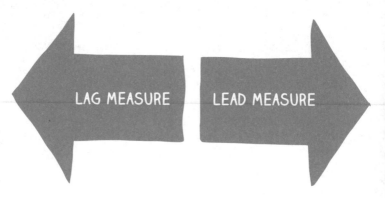

Here are some examples:

Area	Result Required	Lead Measure	Lag Measure
Operational	Referability	Feedback, Order Size, Loyalty	No of referrals
	Staff Loyalty and Reputation	Feedback	Length of Service; Sickness; Recruitment
	Efficiency	Key processes	Efficiency
Financial	Increased Sales	Sales Processes	Sales Numbers
	Costs	Key Controls	Costs

Measurements can be both in the sphere of operations or finance, **but** only when you focus on the **lead** measures will the acceptable **lag** measures follow. In the hyper competitive SR world you can only excel if you focus on the **lead** measures.

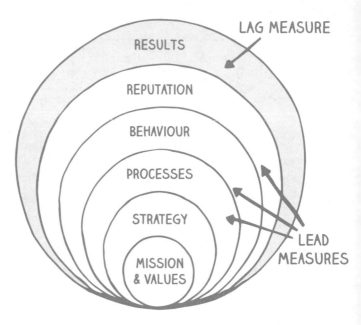

Yes, **lead** measures are more difficult to determine than **lag** indicators. **Lead** measures are **predictive**, i.e. can cost money up front, are open to debate and harder to measure. But reflect on this;

Measuring (lead measures) behaviours, inputs and activities are crucial to the prediction and generation of results, outputs and outcomes.

THINKABOUT 8 - LEAD MEASURES

- Find some GREAT lead measures
- Use them to manage behaviour
- Link them to the lag measures

THIS ALWAYS HELPS - CATCH THEM DOING IT RIGHT!

It's very rare to find a manager who takes genuine notice when something is done well.

If you focus only on negative aspects, then you create a very negative work environment.

Catch them (colleagues, employees), doing things well and provide them with positive feedback. By doing this, you will create a much more positive, stimulating working environment.

FOUR KEY POINTS TO BUILDING YOUR REPUTATION

What is your reputation? Simply put, it is the general beliefs or opinions that are held about **you, your Internal Customers** and therefore **your organization**.

It feels a bit woolly, almost intangible in some respects, but this is everything and if it's good it is something you can take huge pride in.

Here are the four key points that we discussed above, but organized into a system to help you consistently and continually develop and improve your reputation:

Point #1: (Beliefs): Develop **your** Customer Focused Mission
Point #2: (Emotions): Know **your** customer's Real Needs
Point #3: (Actions): Go The Extra Inch
Point #4: (Results): Measure

NUMBER 1
- YOUR CUSTOMER FOCUSED MISSION (CFM)

A 'mission' gives you direction and like a compass keeps you in the right direction when you are lost. A Customer Focused Mission (CFM) expresses **your** beliefs about **your** organization.

Discovering your CFM can be thought of as a FEV(V)ER. You have to continually ask your team "What are we trying to achieve here?"

- **F**ocus: on developing **your CFM** while remembering that **you** will only achieve what you focus on. If you focus on sales then you get them but at the expense of loyal customers. Put customers first and the sales will follow. Focus on delivering **your** customer experience

- **E**mpower: **your** people will only be empowered if they know what's **really** important and they are all aligned in one direction and they make decisions **only** based on the CFM
- **V**ision: you have to have a vision about your organization which is thought through, has passion and is your obsession
- **V**alues: you have to know how you are going to do it, what foundations you are going to put in place
- **E**veryone: it's everyone's responsibility to obsessively ask their customers, and each other, what they think their mission is and therefore discover it
- **R**eal: keep your CFM clear, short and simple. Easy to understand. Make it measurable

In discovering your CFM, think of it as a FEV(V)ER – **it needs to affect everyone in your organization.**

- Be genuine and honest in developing your CFM
- Ensure that you involve everyone in its development. It cannot just be communicated by email

No involvement = No commitment

- Don't confuse it with a corporate mission statement. A CFM involves everyone in its development. Missions can have a bad name as they are often considered just as platitudes
- Remember that a great CFM will be **timeless**

NUMBER 2
- YOUR CUSTOMERS' REAL NEEDS (CRN)

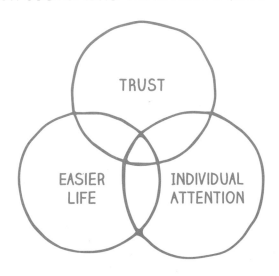

Customers have three overriding emotional needs through any transaction or interaction with **you**:

1. To trust you
2. To have their life made easier or better
3. To get individual attention

Customers are driven by emotion and as a consequence they can:

1. Be unpredictable
2. Have different physical needs
3. Need you to care about them, pay attention to them

But

They all still have similar emotional needs. Customers will always remember how they felt emotionally about your products or services and if you connect with them on an emotional level they will be:

1. Loyal
2. Help you to succeed
3. Promote your goods and services

Words of warning!

The old adage that the 'customer is not always right but they are always a customer' still prevails.

NUMBER 3
- GO THE EXTRA INCH (GTEI)

Your actions will always define you. Success lies in what you do, not what you say. You can take a horse to water but:

- As a manager, you cannot force your people to do anything you tell them to do
- As a salesperson, you cannot get your customers to do what you asked them to do

You can only make them thirsty inch by inch! History shows us that successful evolution only happens and is consolidated inch by inch.

So, the key is to improve your actions by taking small steps, inch by inch and make the steps spectacular rather than trying to do it all in one go ... and fail.

Small steps, taken repeatedly and constantly over time produce great progress. Therefore, make sure your processes are broken down into small steps so that you can repeat them over and over again for consistent and excellent results.

Excellent results can only be delivered through systems and processes that continually evolve and improve to meet the demands of your customers.

NEVER GO THE EXTRA MILE!

Cement the Inches with Accountability, Training and Praise

- By holding people accountable continually and obsessively
- Doing it inch by inch offers more opportunity for praise and celebrating success
- Seeking accreditation for everyone in your organization from certified training bodies and other trade associations reinforces the inches

- Making time for your Internal Customers to grow their skill set increases their value inch by inch
- Rewarding and praising people for their achievements cements your reputation inch by inch.

In doing these actions, your Internal Customers will, positively and without question, refer your organization through their everyday actions and interactions with your customers.

Think about how many times are you impressed by a organization's credentials online or the framed certificates showing their employees skills and achievements on their office wall.

NUMBER 4
- MEASURE

Usually, measurements focus on the results or sales rather than the cause of the result, the customer experience. So, short-term sales are made but at the expense of the customer experience.

That's suicidal, but most organizations try to commit it every day.

It is true to say that:

- What gets measured gets done
- If we can measure something we can improve it (if we can't we won't!)
- Money is only the result of other actions; in order to earn more money, we have to measure the actions that cause customers to want to give it to us

Therefore, to be effective in measuring you have to:

1. **Get your measures right; focus on the lead measures**

2. **Only measure the actions that produce results**

3. **Keep them simple and clear**

4. **Use feedback systems to make sure it happens**

5. **Have clear and compelling public scoreboards**

MEASURE TO EVOLVE

Keeping your reputation is like being on a treadmill and you cannot afford to stop! Your reputation needs to keep fit and it needs to build its resilience against your competitors. It must have the stamina for the long run.

"Keep improving" is a mantra that is repeated in this book without any excuses. There are some good reasons for this:

- Your customers who refer you to others expect to see your products and services continue to evolve and still be of great value for money, because they trust you and are your partners
- If you do not keep improving, your competitors will usurp your market position
- You will lose some team members (and their skills and reputation) if there is no underlying feeling of progression and therefore security

USING A THIRD PARTY FOR FEEDBACK

Don't hesitate to have an external view on setting this up and monitoring. Having an independent opinion is always worthy of consideration because it will help you to:

* Get it right
* Drive the right behaviours
* Add value and perspective
* Send a message that you are serious

SYSTEMS THAT MAKE IT HAPPEN

Many organizations will dabble in some of these areas. They may choose a measure which always puts them in a good light. They may have a customer questionnaire.

However, organizations can only succeed if they systemise these four key processes rigorously in their organizations and put the resources, structure and time in place to facilitate the implementation and evolution of their system.

THE FEEDBACK SYSTEM POWERHOUSE

INVESTORS
IN FEEDBACK

In order to implement the key processes excellently two things must occur:

1. An organization must have a feedback process in order to keep them close to the customers' real needs and continually improve

2. The feedback process must add value to the customer experience and prove that the organization does care

The right feedback system will systematically prove that the organization cares vigorously about the customer and strives to get their products and services right for them, and then follows up.

ENGAGEMENT AND VALUE FIRST

Most sales funnels start with marketing, but a sales process for the SR world, where your sales ability is leveraged either way by your reputation, starts with **engagement and value**, and having these two powerful tools will help to increase:

- **Conversions**
- **Reputation**
- **Referrals**

START BY GATHERING FEEDBACK

Feedback is going to give you more loyalty, higher engagement and more value. It will also give you a competitive edge.

So, if you are consistently gathering feedback you will learn where to make improvements and which inch to focus on.

Then Go the Extra Inch, enhance your competitive edge by engaging with your Internal Customers who love to work for the organizations, those that are continually improving and as a consequence will reward you through their positive actions. They will be **energized** and **empowered** people. They will feel more relaxed in coming forward and are more innovative and supportive.

Keep Moving Forward because however good you are, if you stop improving you will fail. Think about Marks and Spencer. At one stage, they were the third largest retailer in the world, but failed to continually evolve. They are now not even the third largest retailer in the UK. Customers have drifted away from their original core business; they lost customer loyalty, which led to their downfall and they have never really recovered, even with a change of direction.

Your organization will be much more attractive to everyone by doing the four key processes well, the referral cycle will just keep going because in essence your customers become your sales people.

You cannot build your reputation unless you engage with people and add value, simple!

Like everything in life, **it's the order that delivers the value**:

- You can't reap a crop without ploughing and planting it first
- You can't be a professional without an education

And .... Of course ...

- You cannot build your **R**eputation without consistency and continual improvement in your customer experience
- You cannot gain **R**eferrals without a consistently excellent reputation

Period.

If you don't have a **system** you cannot deliver a consistent approach to employees and customers alike.

So in the next chapter, we'll move on to how you can develop a system to make all of this happen.

THINKABOUT 10 - THE ORDER AND SYSTEM: THE 4 KEY PRINCIPLES

- Understand the principles of human behaviour and YOUR Customers' Real Needs
- Engage genuinely and honestly with everyone
- Systemise the four key processes: CFM; CRN; GTEI; Measure
- Rigorous, independent feedback is the powerhouse
- If you don't have a system, you cannot deliver consistent results and improvement ... period

PART THREE

HOW TO 'BE REFERABLE'

FOUR PRINCIPLES OF GETTING REFERRALS

The referral process follows the four common sense principles outlined above: and again they work in sequence. Get the sequence right and you're really on to something, get it wrong and you'll end up in a right muddle.

Here are the four principles:

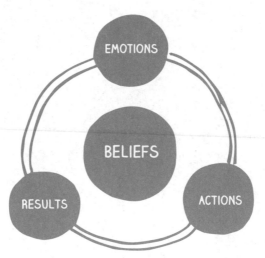

Number 1 – (Beliefs): Be Referable
As we've already discussed, in the age of organization transparency, online reviews that are outside your control, the global market of almost unlimited choice and the demanding empowered customer – everything revolves around being referable. Use the strategy that you learned in the previous chapter to emotionally engage with your customer.

Number 2 – (Emotions): Make it Easy
Make it as easy as possible for customers to refer your organization. Simple is always preferable. Put clear steps and systems in place to make this happen.

Number 3 – (Actions): Keep Improving
Do not make the critical mistake of stopping when you get it right. When referrals start pouring in then it can be tempting to stop. Don't fall prey to that temptation. It looks like everything is going perfectly, so some people will stop listening to customers and stop trying to improve. That is the first step to organization suicide.

Number 4 – (Results): Measure & Respond
Always have a system in place for measuring your referrals. Look for ways to improve your systems. Be sure that you measure where your referrals are coming from. If you know their source and what types of people are most attracted to you, then that will help you moving forward.

As you can see, these four repeating principles drive everything. We can now put them together in one diagram to make life a little clearer!

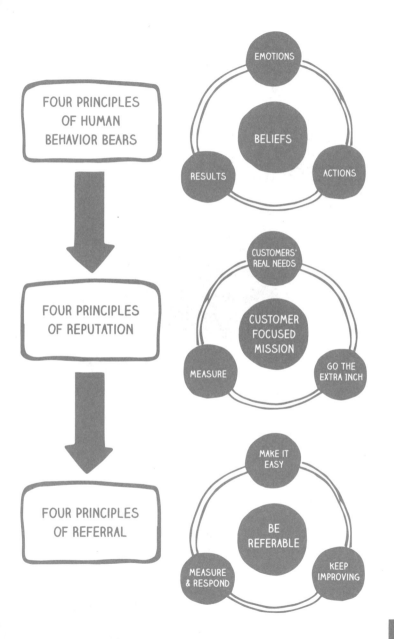

A FEW MORE TIPS FOR MAKING YOUR ORGANIZATION REFERABLE

PEOPLE BUY
FROM PEOPLE
THEY TRUST

People are only going to refer companies that they trust. It takes a lifetime to build trust but only a moment to lose it. You cannot ever let a customer down. For example, if a customer refers someone to you and you don't **give them the best possible** service, then you're not being trustworthy. You have let down both your existing customer and the referral. This is so critical that you need to systemize it so that it's impossible to get it wrong.

Never forget to **thank** a customer for sending you a referral. In fact, put a system in place so that it's impossible to forget to thank them.

Make sure that **existing loyal customers always get better deals than new customers** (excluding limited trial offers).

An example of getting it wrong: a lady noticed that her elderly father's insurance policy renewal cost £400 but when she went online to look at comparable policies, the price was £190 (from the same organization) for a new customer! How could you ever trust this organization again after knowing that they pulled these types of stunt? A legitimate organization would have made the effort to offer the best possible rate to renewal customers rather than keep sapping as much money as possible because they have to pay a marketing organization!

The moral of that story is that you **should never take advantage of having more information than another person** in any situation. If you do, then you're going to end up destroying everyone's trust in you. Remember, bad news spreads faster than good news (and sticks around a lot longer). You can do a thousand things right and spend years building your reputation only to see that reputation crash with just one boneheaded move.

Conclusion: in order to be referable, you have to stick to these four principles in this basic order. Everything that you do should go through those four steps. They are an important check, balance and filter.

THINKABOUT 11 - THE VALUE OF ONE CUSTOMER

- Work out the lifetime value of one typical customer so you get the strength and drive to focus more on customer loyalty, reputation and referrals.

HOW TO GET REFERRALS

So, we've been through the background and foundations to answer the question "how do I get referrals?" Now it's time for the processes, systems and behaviours to actually make this happen!

Let's just examine the four key principles of human behaviour – and your organizational, team, personal and systemic behaviour going forward.

1. BE REFERABLE:
(ALSO CALLED 'CUSTOMER FOCUSED MISSION')

You need to ensure all your organizational, team, personal and systemic behaviour stems from only one belief going forward. Until you have mastered this, don't start trying to do anything else (you'll end up with egg on your face). When you have this clear, then use it every day with all you do:

- The one driver of all strategy
- The basis of every system and process
- The foundation of every meeting
- The ultimate purpose of all training & development
- The fundamental job role of every stakeholder in your organization
- The basis of everything done by everyone all the time

And of course, this belief is:

Our purpose is not to 'make money' – our purpose is to do what we do so well that we are consistently 'referable' – no matter what.

2. 'MAKE IT EASY
(ALSO CALLED 'THE CUSTOMERS' REAL NEEDS')

So now you've got your mind in the right place, you need to ensure that you filter all your organizational, team, personal behaviour systems through the customers' real needs.

The customers' real needs are:

- **Attention**: your organizational, team, and personal behaviour systems need to demonstrate at every step that you genuinely care about the customer as a person – NOT as a number to add money to your bottom line. This splits into two sub areas:

1. **Direct**: your personal dealings: are all your people aligned, trained and held accountable to this?

2. **Indirect**: your systems: are they all filtered through this principle? Do you have aligned systems (especially when things don't go according to plan)? Are all your people empowered to use their common sense to make sure the customer gets the right attention, even if the system says they should do something else? Are you continually improving your systems and processes in this area by gathering feedback and using 'Go the Extra Inch' continual improvement processes (more info on these later)?

- **Easier Life**: your organizational, team, and personal behaviour systems need to be designed with the aim of making your customer's life easier at every step – NOT with the aim of making your organization 'efficient' above all else (by all means be as efficient as you can – but NEVER do this at the expense of making the customer's life harder). This splits into two sub areas:

1. **Physical**: your customer's physical needs: are your organizational, team, and behaviour systems designed to help the customer physically as much as possible; to make the right choice, to easily access services etc.?

2. **Emotional**: your customer's emotional needs: are your organizational, team, and behaviour systems designed to help the customer feel relaxed, cared for and unworried?

- **Trust**: your organizational, team, and personal behaviour systems need to be 100% trustworthy with the aim of establishing unequivocal trust at every step (whether the customer buys from you or not). Not with the aim of making a sale at all opportunities. This splits into two sub areas:

    1. **Competence**: are you experts in your market, and know what your products are best for (and worst for), and what typical needs they fulfil for the customer? Are you well trained in what you do, what your competitors do, what your customers need, what they don't need and what problems they can and have experienced (and how to deal with them). In short: are your professional abilities at all levels top notch?

    2. **Character**: are you genuinely of a trustworthy character? Do you have a clear unequivocal 'customer focused mission' and are you all held accountable to it at all levels? Do you have measures of trustworthy behaviour? Do you proactively seek out feedback? Do you have continual improvement systems in this area? Do you have world class mistake rectification systems? There's a lot to do here!

A great example of getting this wrong has happened as I write this in the beautiful sunny bar of a four-star hotel overlooking the sea in Devon, UK. I ordered a pot of tea but, when it arrived, the very friendly waitress asked for payment, rather than allowing me to open a tab. When I queried this (this is a four-star hotel, not a back street pub), the response was: "We're not allowed to open tabs because people walk out without paying." How did this meet my real needs?

- **Attention**:
  Direct: I don't feel valued at all, I feel mistrusted
  Indirect: the systems are fundamentally negatively affecting customer experience

- **Easy life**
  Physical: my life is made harder as I have to keep paying in small amounts: really inconvenient and unprofessional
  Emotional: I certainly don't feel relaxed or cared for

- **Trust**
  Competence: how incompetent and untrustworthy are they that, after almost 150 years, they can't get a flawless system to sort this problem out?
  Character: how much do they really care about experience and service?

What a four-star cock up!

THINKABOUT 12 - THE CUSTOMERS' REAL NEEDS

- Choose one process per month
- Filter it line by line through the 'Customers' REAL Needs' and then refine it to align with them: one by one

3. 'KEEP IMPROVING'
(ALSO CALLED: 'GO THE EXTRA INCH')

All the above ideas and suggestions sound great in principle, but the key question is: how can we actually make this happen in our organization? After all, you can take a horse to water but you can't make it drink.

And the answer to that is, that you need to do it in small continuous and consistent steps. Inch by inch.

This advice is subject to two conditions:

1. **You** need to have your 'customer focused mission' clear and accepted first.

2. You need a working, world-class 'measure and respond' system (which will signpost the inches that need addressing, every day, every week, every month – you choose the frequency).

The 'Go the Extra Inch' session

The best way to embed the 'Go the Extra Inch' principle into your organization at any level is to use the 'Go the Extra Inch session'. Below is a guide for a standard session. You should not follow this rigidly; instead use the ideas and principles to put in place regular and consistent 'Go the Extra Inch sessions'. This should be wherever you need to use principle 2 ('Make it Easy') to improve your strategy, systems, processes and behaviours. These can be done in person or virtually – or a mix of the two. Here are some suggestions to guide you:

- Weekly team session
- Daily personal session
- Weekly relationship session
- Monthly group session
- Quarterly divisional session
- Ad hoc as needed

Go the Extra Inch Sessions

The group meets as needed. Each person has **two minutes** to answer the following four questions, and be held accountable for progress by their peers (rather than by their manager):

1. **What one thing did I/we do last week that moved us forward an inch?**

2. **What one thing happened this week that was really great, and I want to share with everyone so we can all learn from it?**

3. **What one thing this week was a total mess up, that I want to share so we learn from it and don't repeat it?**

4. **What one thing am I going to do this week to move us, as a team, forward one more inch? What help do I need from other people at this meeting in order to do this? That then ends up being the first agenda item of next week's session, i.e. how did I do on it?**

(Note: point 4 is the single most important point of the meeting – this is where progress in your organization actually happens – but

it's only an inch; Rome wasn't built in a day; don't try and solve issues all in one bite; just look to move forward one inch per week on one issue per person. Small steps done continually, will result in huge progress over time. Anything greater will not happen, and you'll end up with frustration and stop having the sessions.)

It's critically important that you have these meetings. Everyone can see theoretically why this would be such a powerful process, but so often people start this process and then give up because the meetings take too long and can become infuriating!

The way to get around this is for the leader to keep them short and sharp. Get a timer and hold people accountable to the two minutes strictly! Yes, the first few sessions will be a mess, but people will soon get the idea, and then this can become the most powerful process in your organization to drive forward the customer experience.

4. GATHER FEEDBACK FIRST:
(ALSO CALLED: 'MEASURE')
Listening comes first.

You should never put a systematic referral system in place if you do not have a systematic feedback system in place.

You need to be an 'Investor in Feedback'
(for more info please see
www.investorsinfeedback.com)

INVESTORS
IN FEEDBACK

What would happen if you were to ask for a referral from someone who thinks you are rubbish? You didn't get it right for them in the first place. That alone can be forgiven, but by asking them for a referral, you're essentially admitting that you weren't interested in their experience. How good does that look? How angry and vengeful do you think that customer would be?

How much more is this going to anger customers in the future as they begin to realize just how powerful they are?

Your 'Customer Focused Mission' for Feedback
Why would you want to gather feedback in the first place?

The answer lies in your customer focused mission, and it is a good idea in itself to have a customer focused mission specifically for your feedback systems. Perhaps it might look something like this:

We proactively and professionally listen to the opinions of our customers and respond and develop according to what they tell us, so that we can be consistently referable: we do not expect or ask for any referrals until we are convinced we are unquestioningly referable.

So, what happens if you only gather feedback in a blunt (and desperate) attempt to get referrals? The customer will think you're being insincere. They are not stupid and will be able to see right through that.

Indeed, most organizations complain about the ineffectiveness of their referral systems. You know, the ones that usually attempt to bribe you with some kind of reward if you refer them. And of course the real reason for the systems' ineffectiveness is the violation of this principle above.

Customers will not put their own personal credibility on the line and go out of their way for your benefit until they are 100% convinced of your referability, and that you genuinely care about them and about continually being remarkable to them. If there are any exceptions to this rule, the referral is usually more trouble than it's worth because it's been given for the wrong reasons!

Here's a recent example of getting it wrong: I recently received a call from a boiler organization that I had done business with. Here's how that call went:

Organization: "Hello ... I'd like to get some feedback about your recent boiler service."

Me: "No problem."

Organization: "We noticed that your boiler is getting hard to service because it's an older model and the parts are difficult to find. Would you like a quote on a new one?"

What's wrong with that example? Everything!

They started the call by asking me if I could provide feedback, but did they ever ask for feedback? No! They weren't interested in gathering feedback. They were trying to make a sale. They immediately lost my trust because they lied to me. Why would I buy from them when I don't trust them?

What would happen if they got it right and gathered feedback properly?

They could have ended the call with something like, "By the way, we noticed that your boiler is getting old. How would you like us to come out and give you a no obligation quote?" I probably would have said "yes."

However, they violated my real needs so I told them "no."

(And that means 'no' forever – not just now)

Don't use feedback to try to sell things, use feedback as a powerful process in itself.

How to do it right:

- ✓ Make it easy for the customer to give you feedback.
- ✓ Proactively call them to gather feedback
- ✓ Build trust by doing it really, really well

Your feedback system must be based on an inch-by-inch approach. What I mean is that you don't ask for everything all at once. Furthermore, you need to improve it inch by inch as well.

Where do these inches come from to move your organization forward? The inches come from the feedback as you continually improve it.

THINKABOUT 13 - *'GREAT OR POOR'*

- Buy and read Guy Arnold's *Great or Poor*, which explores these four principles in detail and gives you many more hints and tips to use them in your everyday activities for consistent progress towards 'greatness' and 'referability'

HOW TO EFFECTIVELY GATHER FEEDBACK

INVESTORS
IN FEEDBACK

We've talked about the principles of gathering feedback so it's time to put that knowledge to use. Here's how you take action to actually gather feedback.

There are two things that we have to note before we begin.

1. The feedback system used depends on the relationship that you have with the customer. Whether it's transactional, emotional, relationship or an ongoing partnership.

HORSES FOR COURSES

CUSTOMER RELATIONSHIP

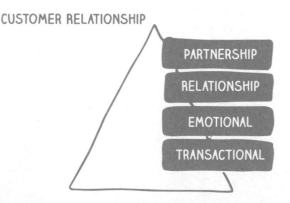

PARTNERSHIP

RELATIONSHIP

EMOTIONAL

TRANSACTIONAL

More on this later.

2. All feedback must follow a very clear formula.
   Receiving and collecting feedback can be a very delicate process. It can be personal and difficult for both parties. Without the right formula there is a significant risk that you could mess this up and jeopardize the whole relationship in the process.

To explain this process in an easy way, let's use the following phone call conversation as an example.

Introduction:

EXAMPLE 1
"Hello Mr Arnold. I see you had an engineer out at your place last week. This is a courtesy call to see how it went and to ask if there was anything we could have done better. Is now a good time to talk?"

EXAMPLE 2
"Hello Mr Arnold. I see you had an engineer out at your place last week. This is a courtesy call to find out what you think. Would you be prepared to talk to us now or could we talk at another time?"

There are several points made in these examples:

1. It's a courtesy call
2. The call starts with open questions
3. Permission is requested before moving forward

If they say "no" to giving you feedback, then that's perfectly okay. You will never get 100% of your customers to provide feedback (but you can always ask everyone).

EXAMPLE (IF THEY ANSWER "NO")
"OK, no problem: could we perhaps talk at another time?"

If "yes" you can then rearrange the call.

EXAMPLE (IF THEY ANSWER "NO")
"That's absolutely fine but can I leave you with a (contact details). If you have any feedback or queries, then you can get in touch."

They are very likely to answer "yes" to this question. In fact, I would say that if you did everything perfect up to this point then 100% of customers will answer "yes" to this question.

Your goal is to make life easy for customers. You are not going to ever be able to get 100% of them to provide feedback but you should still thank them for their time. After all, they took the call.

We will now assume that they agreed to provide feedback, so once they've said "yes," then you need to trigger them with OPEN questions like:

- ✓ How was your experience in general?
- ✓ What, if anything, could we have done better?
- ✓ How happy are you with your experience?

However, do not just read off a list of questions. You should not have a script in front of you to read from. You have to ask in a conversational way like in the examples above.

When hiring people to do this, they need to have outstanding communication skills. They need to be very good at listening and building empathy with people. A process that is often called 'peeling the onion'.

What will generally happen is that the customer will then start talking willingly, openly and on their own terms. You don't have to trigger them more: they will tell you what they want to tell you. If they do, then your job is simply to listen to them, take notes, ask open questions (to peel the onion) and to **do the job properly.**

What you want to know is irrelevant because that's only important to you. What is important to your customer is more significant than what is important to you.

This seems obvious but so many people get it wrong and the consequences could be disastrous:

- The customer feels abused
- The process makes the relationship with the customer worse
- You fail to find out the specific issues that need addressing
- You miss trends in what customers are thinking
- You miss the areas your customer experience needs tweaking

You just go with what your customer wants to say. Then you peel the onion by asking certain questions.

✓ How did that happen?
✓ What happened there?
✓ How did you feel about that?
✓ Who did that?
✓ When did that happen?
✓ I don't fully understand, can you tell me more?

These should all be open questions. If you train your people right then this process will run smoothly, train them wrong and you'll end up with poor information and a big muddle!

Note: as you become more and more skilful at this process, you can change the angle of these questions to finding out your customer's opinion on particular areas of your business (e.g.: delivery, phone service). But you must never lead the customer in your direction, you can only find out when they have satisfactorily told you what are the vital areas to them (and what they think about these areas), otherwise you risk leading your customer off track and getting the negative consequences listed above.

THINKABOUT 14 - EMPATHIC LISTENING

- Practice opening lines that are engaging and considerate
- Practice asking open questions and listening with empathy
- Research empathic listening on YouTube and train yourself

RECORDING FEEDBACK

INVESTORS IN FEEDBACK

Once you start getting feedback you will need a way to record it. More importantly, it needs to be recorded in an organised and useful way.

We recommend that you create a spreadsheet and add rows for key items. The purpose of this spreadsheet is to collect information from your customers so you can use it effectively.

You can also build a list of things that you feel are essential to your organization and then compare that list to what the customer feels is key to your organization.

Customer feedback, done properly, is by its nature random. So you will need a good system that enables you to make sense of this feedback.

The spreadsheet could look something like this:

Customer Name			
We're Good At			
We're Not Good At			
Specific Subject 1			
Specific Subject 2			
Specific Subject 3			
General Comments			
Score (out of 10)			

You could add more rows but remember that the more rows you include, the more difficult it is to differentiate and clarify. The customer is going to be talking conversationally while this information is being recorded so it's important to keep it simple!

Not every customer is going to talk about the same things. There is going to be a mixture of topics between customers. What a customer talks about most is going to be the most important items to them personally, so you want to make sure that you can capture their 'good' and 'not good' comments first. You can then easily evaluate the data later and put the most focus on items that customers bring up the most.

Too many companies are heavily reliant on online surveys for feedback. What can a customer really tell you with an online survey? Not a lot – not nearly as much as they can from a simple phone call. There's no option for the customer to tell you how important something is when they do an online survey. There's no way for them to discuss issues that are not included on the survey.

If you're not going to do feedback properly then it's better not to do it at all.

Because poorly executed feedback:

- Gives dangerously inaccurate information
- Annoys customers
- Wastes time and money
- Generates no loyalty and referrals

If you set up this system correctly, the spreadsheet will show you:

- What's most important to your customers
- What's happening in the market
- How you're doing against your competition
- What other options they had and have
- What to stop doing
- What to start doing
- What to continue doing

These will then lead you into an opportunity to systematically gather referrals and introductions – more on this later.

You can also use this information to catch your people doing things well. It's important that you don't just use this information to beat up people. If you just use feedback for this then you are making it a negative activity. Instead, you want the process of gathering feedback to be a positive activity. You want people to get value out of this and want more of it.

There is also a tiny row at the bottom of the spreadsheet (I'm sure you noticed it). This row is where you will enter the score. You're on the phone with your customer and they have given you their feedback. You've listened and recorded it into the spreadsheet. Once the call is coming to an end, you ask them:

✓ Would it be OK to ask two more questions?

If they say "no," that's fine. Thank them and end the call on a positive note. But, in our experience, 98% of customers will agree to this – provided you've done the listening and onion peeling well.

If they say "yes" here are the two questions:

1. If you had to rate your experience on a scale of 10, what score would you give?

2. (See below for the 2nd question: it will depend on the answer to the first one!)

You're trying to narrow this feedback down into a score. The ability to measure your service with a number gives you the ability to improve it. Here's how you use that grade:

9-10	Great
7-8	Satisfactory
6 or lower	Poor

Note: many people and organizations think that 'satisfactory' is OK – it isn't. 'Satisfied' customers will not be loyal to you (there's an 80% chance they'll use someone else's services next time, and they certainly won't spread your reputation or recommend you). If you have customers that are merely 'satisfied', then you're in real trouble and will have to compete through special offers and expensive marketing. A good example of this happening in practice can be seen in the expensive and inefficient way most supermarkets compete with each other. So never ask if people are 'satisfied' and never seek 'customer satisfaction' as it has no value.

THERE'S NO SUCH THING AS 'BAD' FEEDBACK

YOU CAN'T LOSE

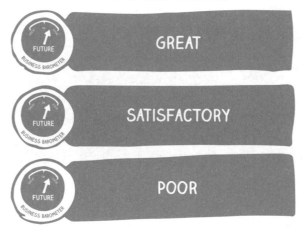

A lot of people and articles talk about 'bad' feedback, but in reality, there is no such thing as 'bad' feedback. There is only feedback handled badly! The key to making feedback work and pay huge dividends for you lies in how you react and respond to it:

- If the feedback is 'great': you can put in systems and permission to cross sell, up-sell, get referrals and build your reputation.
- If the feedback is 'satisfactory': you can get permission to contact them and build the relationship further. This gives you the

opportunity to turn it into 'great' (because, as explained above, 'satisfied' customers aren't good enough).

- If the feedback is 'poor': you can put your crisis management process into operation and blow their socks off. Sometimes poor feedback handled excellently presents the greatest opportunity to build reputation, referrals, and loyalty. However, 'poor' feedback should be treated as an emergency and you have to act immediately on it (obviously!)
- More information on all this shortly.

THINKABOUT 15 - BLOW THEIR SOCKS OFF RESPONSE

- Start thinking about 'blow their socks off' responses to feedback that will significantly enhance the relationship and make them feel genuinely listened to and valued

OFTEN, IT'S BEST PRACTICE TO USE A THIRD PARTY TO GATHER, OR ACCREDIT AND AUDIT YOUR FEEDBACK PROCESS

INVESTORS IN FEEDBACK

Here are the 10 key reasons why you should consider using a third-party customer experience specialist to help you execute, audit or accredit this process.

1. **Honesty.** The customer just wants to tell you what they think, honestly, without embarrassment or upset. The only way you can be sure of this is via a third party, since they can't solve, they can only listen.

2. **Provides perspective.** The third party will see the feedback just as it is, and will be able to see the issues clearly and from an unbiased but expert perspective. No matter how objective you think you are, you'll filter all customer feedback through your own emotions and desires.

3. **Cost-effective use of time and resources.** Your expertise lies in providing your service. Using a third party to collate and provide customer feedback is both cost effective in time, and avoids distraction and bias. Your energies are best spent using the feedback to improve your organization – not gathering it.

4. **Ensures integrity to the customer's needs and desires.** Again, no matter how objective you are, you won't be able to resist the odd extra question here and there. This will destroy the exercise in the customer's view. The customer just wants you to listen to them – nothing else!

5. **High response rates.** If you're paying for the service, you'll want to use it as much as possible. If you do it yourself it'll just be a chore and your mindset will be the opposite.

6. **Regular report with a score.** Only a third party can give you an objective score which can be used to motivate and encourage your people. Only a third party will always produce a full report – if you do it yourself, you may be tempted to cut corners in these vital areas.

7. **Peace of mind.** Using a third party ensures it gets done on time every time.

8. **Resource.** Using a customer service specialist means that you'll benefit from their input and resources to help you.

9. **Shows you're serious.** Using a third party shows that you really do want to know what your customer thinks, and that you're prepared to invest money and time to do this. As long as it's done right, it seriously impresses the customer and builds loyalty.

10. **Public credibility.** if you use a third party for this exercise you can openly publish your score with integrity and credibility. Done right this can add massive value to your brand and customer trust.

RESPONDING TO FEEDBACK

Now you have started gathering feedback effectively, you need to respond to it effectively.

Just remember:

'Gathering feedback effectively is vital, responding to it effectively is dynamite!'

So far in our system you have:

1. Demonstrated high levels of genuine care by gathering feedback proactively

2. Made the customer feel valued by listening well

3. Discovered what the customer does and doesn't like about you

4. Learned other things you could be doing to please customers better in the future

5. Learned what your competition is doing/why your customer chose/didn't choose you, etc...

All very valuable. But now, you're going to respond to the feedback – a process we call 'Elastic and Velcro Marketing', and this will turn this feedback into pure gold. It will:

- Systemize referrals, reputation and recommendations from loyal customers
- Supercharge cross and up selling
- Help you develop better relationships and more loyalty from 'satisfied' customers (and turn them into 'loyal' customers)
- Rescue unhappy customers effectively

Not bad for a simple system!

Note: all this has another massive benefit in your organization. As soon as you put a measure into your system that holds your employees personally accountable, they will raise their game significantly. Just be sure that when you first share the feedback with them that you share the positive first. You can address the negative once you have reviewed the positive. This is much more a carrot than a stick. Use public scoreboards for all feedback, team and individual. If you gave a clear and compelling scoreboard, no one will want to be on it for a negative reason!

ELASTIC AND VELCRO MARKETING

As we continue with the feedback process, the second question will depend on how they answered the first question.

You should by now be shifting your focus from marketing to customer experience (reputation and referability). We want these people to come back and we want them to bring others with them. If you have done everything up to this point correctly, you are now able to move into the area of loyalty and referrals.

With that said, the next question depends on the feedback that a customer gave.

Question 2: If they scored you as 'great' – choose one of the following:

- Would you be willing to refer our services?
- Would you be willing to introduce us to (suitable people)?
- Would you be willing to write us a review on ...?

If a customer gave you a score of 9 or 10, then most of them are going to answer "yes" to this question. You have blown their socks off with your services and feedback system. However, the problem is that while most will agree to refer you, only a small percentage will actually do it if you don't actively make it happen. Your goal is to increase that percentage.

You can achieve this by being completely open with the customer. Explain that your organization tries to get new customers through direct referrals and how this will benefit everyone.

Be completely transparent. Customers will want to help people they like!

"We focus on getting direct referrals because it helps both of us. It keeps marketing costs down so that we can focus more on providing the best products/services at the best possible price."

Once that introduction is done, then you ask the real question:

"If we called you in a week or so, would you be willing to give us one name or phone number that you'd be happy to refer us directly to?"

Remember, we're using an inch-by-inch approach.

Only ask for one referral. If they can and want to give you more, this won't stop them, but by only asking for one, you're not trespassing on their goodwill and they're much more likely to want to help you – it's polite! Also, make sure that you say this in a way that makes it easy for them to say "no" because you don't want them to get uncomfortable.

If they answer "no," then that's fine. Politely thank them, ask for permission to gather feedback from them again in the future, and end the call. Remember, this is a marathon, not a sprint.

If they do agree to allow you to call back in a week then you have to make sure that you follow through with your promise. If you don't, then you will have lost their trust.

When you call back a week later, one of two things will happen:

1. They will not be ready. They haven't even thought about it at all. You have to be polite.

"Okay. What would you like me to do? Would you like me to leave it or phone you back?"

They will probably tell you to "phone them back" because they have given you a promise. In general, people do not like to break their promises. In that case, make sure that you phone them back in a week. Again, you never want to break your word.

2. They will have a referral ready for you.

"Yes! I've spoken to Tom. Here is his number."

And of course, another thing that can happen quite regularly is that they might give you more than one referral.

FOOD FOR THOUGHT
Imagine if every other customer throughout a year were to give you a referral. Out of those referrals, 30% of them were to become customers:
That's a 15% increase in business for virtually no cost.

You could also alternatively offer a special service or club to these customers

You can form an inner circle group and give some of these customers an invitation to join. These inner circles work much better than most marketing campaigns.

Note: it's VITALLY important to ensure that these special offers definitely are special (better than you offer anywhere else) and exclusive (not available anywhere else): you want this 'club' to have real exclusivity and value, and you definitely want to avoid looking untrustworthy by getting this wrong!

Consider setting up special events for these members. Send them a special offer then always inform them that they can bring one friend – **but only one friend**.

Why only one? Because then it's

- Limited
- Exclusive
- Special
- And therefore, very desirable.

If done well, this works a treat in practice. For example, a small hotel chain in the UK increased bookings by over 25%, room rate by over 10%, and reduced marketing costs by 50% all by operating this system.

Using 'greats' to improve your reputation.

Great feedback also gives you the opportunity to build your reputation systematically with a special place where they can give you an online review.

Online review gathering example:

> "Thanks so much for giving us feedback. If we sent you a link to our [web review] page by email would you be willing to leave us a short review?"

Some people will agree with this and some won't. It's not a big deal if they don't and you never want to put pressure on your customers. In our experience, about 30–40% of them will say yes. Thirty per cent is a lot more than none at all, which is what you will get if you never ask.

Great feedback gives you a lot of potential that you should tap into.

The reason why collecting feedback should, at least in the first instance, be carried out on a one-by-one basis is so that you can try out new things if you want to. You can set up two systems and run each one for a month to determine which of those systems works best. Just remember that the basics are always going to be the same. That's it for great feedback.

Question 2: When the customer marks you as 'satisfactory', try to build the relationship

'Satisfactory' isn't great, but it's also not an emergency. You should address it as follows:

"Would it be okay for a director of the organization to call you within a week to listen to you a bit more so that they will know what is needed to improve our relationship?"

They will almost always answer "yes" to this question because there is absolutely no risk to them.

It's important that you have a break between this call and the follow-up call though. What happens if you were gathering feedback and then went straight in to try and fix it right then?

THERE ARE NO SHORTCUTS TO ANY PLACE WORTH GOING

You did not ask for permission to resolve the problem, so they will almost definitely see it as bad manners, and they will slay you.

Remember, you were only given permission to call for feedback. It was not for an in-depth phone call. You have to get permission to build the relationship.

- Diagnosis First
- Resolution Second
- No Short Cuts!

It's all about manners!

Question 2: When they mark you as 'poor', try to salvage the relationship

'Poor' is not a reason to panic. It's definitely an emergency but you can still salvage it. Indeed, you're in a very good place to salvage it, because you approached them, they didn't have to go out of their way to complain to you.

You actually have a great chance to blow their socks off by showing them that you are willing to go above and beyond in order to salvage your relationship with them.

Making an effort now will show them that they are important to you.

Your response should be something like this:

> "This sounds terrible. Our director will definitely want to ring you quickly. Is it okay for me to send her this feedback immediately and for her to get back to you by the end of the day tomorrow so that she can try to sort this out for you?"

Again, you have to put some kind of break between the feedback call and the resolution call. However, the break needs to be short with 'poor' feedback because you are in salvage mode. Time is definitely of the essence! And now you've raised their expectations by your world class feedback system and reacting positively to bad feedback, don't blow it all by reacting slowly!

Then all you need to do is put your world class problem resolution system in place and systematically not only salvage the situation, but, of course, also blow their socks off by the fantastic way you do this.

TAKE SMALL STEPS

When you receive feedback from a customer, it's important to always take small steps. Follow these three essential tips:

1. Make it easy for them
2. Never make it an inconvenience for them
3. Always be polite

Why Is Elastic and Velcro Marketing So Effective?

Consider this for a moment. What kind of response do you normally get when you give feedback?

Nothing at all! You're lucky if you even get a "thank-you".

They might be acting on your feedback but you have absolutely no way of knowing. So, you have gone out of your way in your busy schedule to take time to give them feedback, and it's disappeared into a black hole. What a waste of time and effort! You won't bother to do that again (and you'll look at their competitors next time you need what they supply). Disastrous!

What I'm suggesting to you is that you operate your organization using a very specific type of system.

One to make yourself remarkable and referable!

THINKABOUT 16 - ELASTIC AND VELCRO MARKETING

- Start thinking about your 'Elastic and Velcro Marketing' system
- Use these words (everyone will ask what you're on about)
- Test and measure different next steps for your 'great' feedbacks
- Follow the steps closely for your 'satisfactory's and 'poor's

THINKABOUT 17 - WE BOOBED

- Check your problem resolution system
- Make sure it follows the four "Great or Poor" principles
- Make sure everyone is empowered and trained expertly
- Test and measure it constantly: get help from experts
- Listen continually for problems: they'll show you where the cracks are

REMEMBER 'LAPSED' CUSTOMERS ARE 'NOT NOWS'

Ok, so now you have a

* World class proactive feedback system, and
* A world class Elastic and Velcro Marketing system

You've made a great start!

When you've got these two systems running well, then please make sure you extend them to:

* Your lapsed customers
* Your lost customers
* Your not nows (potential customers who aren't buying from you yet)
* Your suppliers

And, most importantly of all, your people (your Internal Customers)

All these people are a massive potential source of information. They are in a position to help you to continually improve and have innovative ideas – don't ignore them!

But beware that these types of feedback can be more delicate than 'standard' customer feedback. For this reason we also recommend that these types are best carried out by an independent professional third party on your behalf.

And note that in addition to the huge value you can get from the feedback in its own right, this type of feedback can also have massive elastic and velcro outcomes, if handled properly:

- Your lapsed customers can be re-engaged
- Your lost customers can be re-won
- Your not nows can become active customers
- Your suppliers can be a huge source of help with regards to competition, innovation and ideas, and potential referrals
- And, most importantly of all, your people will help you get your systems and processes aligned around your customer focused mission and your customers' real needs

This is an exercise worth investing time, money and energy in continually!

THINKABOUT 18 - OTHER STAKEHOLDER FEEDBACK

- Identify your 'other stakeholders'
- Work on one at a time to set up a world class feedback and 'Elastic and Velcro Marketing' system

THE FOUR LEVELS OF CUSTOMER RELATIONSHIPS

Gathering feedback is vital as we know, but it's how you respond to it that really matters. If you're not planning on responding to feedback then it's not worth getting it in the first place! Ninety-five per cent of organizations fall into this category at the moment, so you could set yourself seriously ahead of the game, by understanding this issue and getting it right: this is a major opportunity! Feedback that you don't respond to proves to the customer that you don't really care.

HORSES FOR COURSES

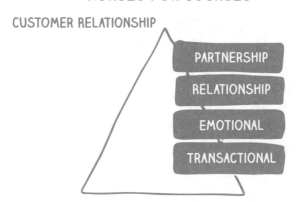

CUSTOMER RELATIONSHIP

PARTNERSHIP

RELATIONSHIP

EMOTIONAL

TRANSACTIONAL

Not all customer relationships are the same, remember, we mentioned this earlier. There are four main types of customer relationship.

What you should be trying to do with your customers is two things:

1. Know your relationship and apply the principles in the right way for that relationship

2. Move your customer up steps to cement the relationship and build true loyalty over time

Here's a basic explanation of the four different levels:

1. **Transactional:** for transactions, e.g. basic purchases

2. **Emotional:** for more emotional purchases, e.g. leisure activities, upmarket purchases and fashion

3. **Relationship:** for relationship purchases, e.g. B2B, and memberships

4. **Partnership:** where your customer actively works to help you build your organization – which results in your organization skyrocketing!

Many organizations only focus on transactional, which is the bottom level on the triangle. That was fine during the Industrial Age but in today's SR world that's simply not going to cut it. In the world of the empowered customer, open reviews and social media you can't afford to have customers any less than emotionally engaged.

The higher up the triangle you take your customer routinely, the more likely they are to:

- Buy again
- Buy larger amounts
- Cross purchase other goods and services
- Be fiercely loyal, even when your competitors are perhaps cheaper
- Actively recommend you to others
- Give you lots of leeway when you get it wrong and tell you quickly

Let's look at the four levels and how feedback relates to each one.

THE FOUR LEVELS OF FEEDBACK

TRANSACTIONAL FEEDBACK

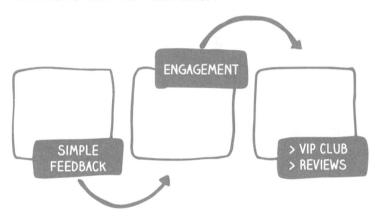

Transactional feedback is best known as 'product reviews'. Transactional feedback can be gathered online with forms. For example, if you buy a new battery for your phone and you fill out a quick form to review that purchase. If you have ever shopped on eBay, you know that you are allowed to rate your transaction. This is transactional feedback.

Transactional feedback is best gathered and displayed online while asking for direct contact and/or resolution by email if there are any issues. Online reputation is the most powerful marketing tool for this type of customer relationship.

These customers can be 'moved up the triangle': please see the matrix at the end of this section for guidance of what to do to achieve this.

EMOTIONAL FEEDBACK

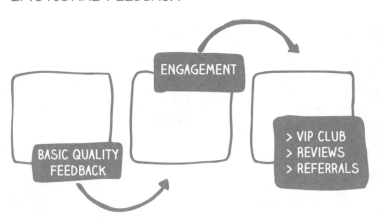

Emotional Feedback is from a much more emotionally involved purchase, often a discretionary one, and often one that has an impact on the customer's image or ego. So, it has to be more interactive than transactional feedback. An online form alone is not going to cut it. This type of feedback can be done by telephone but there are also text or customer response or letter systems for gathering it.

Example 1: if you own a holiday cottage then you could send out two separate text messages.

Text 1: When the customer arrives, a text message welcomes them while serving as a friendly reminder of the housekeeper's phone number. You would also inform the customer that she will be receiving a text when she leaves that will ask for feedback (and why it is so helpful and what you'll do with it).

Text 2: When they leave, you send a text asking her for feedback.

Example 2: if you're running a hotel, you could call every customer within 24 hours after they have left, by phone (using the system outlined above) for genuine feedback. This works like a dream!

These customers can be 'moved up the triangle': please see the matrix at the end of this section for guidance of what to do to achieve this.

RELATIONSHIP FEEDBACK

This is the next step up from emotional feedback. It's based on a longer-term relationship of mutual trust. We suggest this is best done by phone. The wonderful thing about phone calls is that:

- You're distant enough to not make them feel uncomfortable
- You can listen to their tone of voice and other 'body language' signals. So much more information can be satisfactorily conveyed

Many organizations have massive resources invested into phone systems that are designed to get new customers. Yet few of them are investing money into building their relationships with existing customers. Fools!

In fact, it's not even expensive to set up a phone system for this purpose. You can spend half an hour per day on this and get some truly amazing results.

The absolute worst thing that could happen is that you are forced to leave them a message. In that case, you can simply leave them the information needed to contact you. Just by genuinely attempting to make the connection you are showing your customers that you really do care.

Getting all this right gives your organization a huge edge over the competition. But you must be genuine!

We operate this same phone system to gather feedback for customers as well as gathering it for ourselves. The most common feedback that we get from customers is, "Wow! Thanks for calling... these people obviously really do care." They are blown away because we have a system set up that is genuinely interested in their feedback and is not trying to sell them anything. They are also blown away because so few others are doing it, and certainly not doing it properly!

Divert marketing budget from finding new customers and put it into setting up a great feedback system. It will make your life so much easier, your results so much better. Your customers will absolutely love it!

You can then reap the rewards of systematic referrals and easier selling through enhanced reputation. These customers can be moved up the triangle, please see the matrix at the end of this section for guidance of what to do to achieve this.

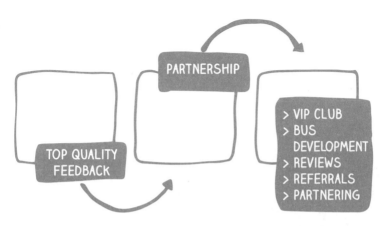

PARTNERSHIP FEEDBACK

Partnership feedback pertains to the Holy Grail of R&R: this is feedback from long term B2B relationships,that helps you develop and grow with your customers, in partnership. You have to use the phone to gather this type of feedback.

Partnership is also the word we'd use to describe the 'nirvana relationship' that fiercely loyal relationship customers have to top brands and suppliers. They are partners because they have a win/win symbiotic relationship.

These partners can actively help each other by:

- Giving proactive feedback
- Helping each other succeed
- Sharing information on marketplaces and competitor activity
- Cross promoting
- Working together on projects
- And so on...

Feedback gathering in these situations has to be handled very carefully and has to be put together in a bespoke way, depending on the relationship and situation. It should always be done by a high quality third party, and should be very discrete. It should be done to enhance the partnership.

| Relationship | Partnership | Relationship | Emotional | Transactional |
Move to	Partnership	Partnership	Relationship	Emotional
Make Feedback Easy		X	X	X
Respond to all Feedback and Use Elastic & Velcro Marketing		X	X	X
Proactively Take Issues offline		X	X	X
Create VIP Customer Offers	X	X	X	X
Create VIP Groups	X	X	X	
Create Specialist Buying Groups	X	X		
Offer Complementary Products or Services	X	X	X	X
Partner with Complementary Products or Services	X	X		
Be Upfront and Proactive in your statements about wanting them to be delighted	X	X	X	X
Look for Issues before they Arise	X	X	X	
Gather Online Reviews from Happy Customers			X	X
Proactively gather Feedback using a Customer Focused System	X	X	X	X
Work as a Win/Win Partnership	X			

HOW TO GET IT WRONG

A solicitor was considering how their feedback system could be improved. The first consideration here should be if they were doing anything to gather feedback.

Yes – they were sending out a letter to customers after the work had been completed. That letter included a feedback form that the customer could fill out and return. But only 20% of these forms were being returned! Essentially, they had no idea what the majority of their customers thought about their services. Twenty per cent is actually a good return rate for a form but 80% is the number that really stands out. That's a huge amount of lost potential, and a lot of dangerous guessing.

"What do the other 80% think about your services?"

My point here is that you have to know what your customers are thinking. You can't just assume that the majority of your customers are happy; otherwise you're making a monumental assumption. Assumptions are dangerous!

Getting back to our example above, the solicitor should ask themselves, if a new customer gets in touch, would I phone them back or send them a form to fill in? The answer should be to phone them back of course.

"So why are you treating new customers better than your existing ones?"

THINKABOUT 19 - FEEDBACK SYSTEMS

- Start thinking about designing the best possible feedback system for your situation
- It doesn't have to be expensive, but it does have to be genuine
- And remember these principles:
  - You're gathering feedback, not solving problems
  - Treat existing customers better than new ones
  - Be prepared to invest a bit of money and time in doing this properly: it's MUCH more cost effective than marketing yourself to potential new customers
  - Be prepared to bring in a professional third party to help you get this right

THIRD-PARTY ONLINE REVIEWS

You're doing really well and you now have:

- A world class proactive feedback system, and
- A world class 'Elastic & Velcro Marketing' system

If you do this properly, professionally, continually and obsessively, with your key stakeholders, and you take effective 'go the extra inch' actions from all these great gold nuggets, you'll be well on your way to having a world class system. You will ensure you are consistently remarkable and referable – most of the hard work is done!

But what about those other niggly online reviews? The ones:

- You're not proactively gathering
- Outside your direct influence
- Unfiltered and unaccredited
- Fair and unfair

These are the ones on third-party review sites and social media.

How can you not only deal effectively with these, but also use them to help you improve and prosper, which is the desired result of all feedback and reviews.

The first thing to do is to make sure you see them in the right way. They may be unfair, inconsistent, scurrilous and perhaps even libellous. Of course, on the flip side, they may be fair, flattering and fantastic, but you **cannot fight them**.

I think it helps to think of King Cnut here: don't try and turn back the tide – you'll lose! What I mean is that this will happen, whether you like it or not, you cannot control or stop it. If you try to, then you'll waste huge amounts of time and energy that could be put to much better use. Instead I suggest you remember the following principles, and take the following steps:

Principles:

1. **There is no such thing as bad feedback (or publicity) – it's how you respond to it that determines the outcome.**

2. **There is no such thing as an unimportant customer, treat every customer like a VIP and you'll be fine.**

3. **If you don't respond to any feedback, in any reader's eyes this will show that you don't care.**

4. **The quality and style of your response demonstrates your personality and principles to the world. It's PR, not one to one problem resolution.**

Example of getting this very right:

- **Bodyform's brilliant response to a viral Facebook complaint**

After an irritated boyfriend posted a 'complaint' on the Bodyform Facebook page, Bodyform took to the internet to issue a spoof apology, with an actress playing the organization's mock chief executive: Caroline Williams.

She explains in a highly amusing spoof way that Bodyform was 'just trying to protect men from the real truth about women's bodies'.

Both the comment and the response went viral, and Bodyform's sales figures went in the right direction too ... thus turning a 'negative online review' into a massive PR and marketing triumph.

Example of getting this very wrong:

- The 'United Breaks Guitars' story we looked at earlier: where United reacted badly to a YouTube video complaint (and suffered stock price drop of around 10% in consequence)

RESPONDING TO THIRD-PARTY ONLINE FEEDBACK

There's a lot of talk about bad online reviews, and the negative affect they can have on a organization, and, indeed many acres of print have been devoted to legal routes and fighting them. But there is a better response that works to:

- Reduce stress and time
- Improve your PR whether the review is good or bad
- Help turn any review into extra business

These ideas have been adopted by leading organization operators across the UK, including top and award winning organizations... and they work.

So, what's the secret and what do we do about these bad reviews?

There are four steps:

1. Accept that the world has changed and the customer really is in charge.
   - Social media and online review sites have empowered the customer like nothing before. This is a genuine revolution in consumer behaviour, not a fad
   - Don't try to swim against the tide, it's pointless and frustrating
   - Remember the potential for success in this new customer empowered market. You see them every day in the news, eBay, Airbnb, Uber etc

2. Genuinely put the desire to be remarkable and referable at the heart of all you do.

3. Put proactive feedback systems in place
   - Don't wait for the review to appear on TripAdvisor or Google. By then it's too late!
   - If you don't proactively demonstrate to the customer that you really do care and really do want their feedback, they'll assume (usually correctly) that you don't

- You must put proactive feedback systems in place to help them tell you what you need to know. These will vary according to the organization.

4. React strongly and positively to all public online reviews. Remember that there's no such thing as a bad online review.
   - The key point is that you are not responding to the individual, you are demonstrating your personality to the world. This is free PR and marketing, pure and simple
   - Calm your ego, customers are not always right, but they are always the customer!
   - Respond to all reviews, otherwise it looks like you don't care. This is VERY important
   - Customers are three times more interested in your response than the review. They know that people can be awkward: what they're interested in is what you're like when you respond!
   - Negative reviews are read five times more than positive reviews. So, responding to these properly is a HUGE opportunity

Negative reviews fall into two categories, valid and false.

For valid reviews, take it on the chin, ask them to contact you offline. State publicly what you aim to be great at and how brilliantly you would have handled this complaint if it had been made direct to you at the time. Free publicity for how trustworthy you are and how great is your problem resolution system.

For false reviews, treat them exactly the same: ask them politely and kindly to contact you offline, state your commitment to great customer experiences (and all the steps that you're taking every day to make this a genuine reality), apologize for what needs apologizing for. Then you should state what you DO do and DON'T do (e.g.: you don't need to apologize for not doing something that is well outside your key business) ... and why this is. Next you should state what you would have done if they had brought this to your attention at the time, and reiterate your commitment to feedback and wanting to get it right for the customer. If you can manage it, add a little humour throughout: the reader will pick it up – after all, fun people are likeable people!

A Six-step Process to Make It REALLY Easy:

1. Stop and take a deep breath: remember the principles.

2. Review the feedback.
   a. What is valuable that you need to take hold of and use to power your 'Go the Extra Inch' systems?
   b. What is perhaps overcooked?

3. Prepare a response as if you were dealing with the most valuable customer you have, face to face.

4. Get a dispassionate colleague (or third-party adviser) to review the response.

5. Improve it until it complies with your customer focused mission and the customer's real needs.

6. Post it. Make sure you urge the original customer to contact you offline to solve the specific instance.

If you manage all the above systems well, you should also get many more positive reviews online. That's great. It's free marketing to the people who are interested. Fantastic!

So, there's no such thing as bad reviews, and, by the way, there's no such thing as bad feedback either. **It's how you respond to it that makes all the difference.**

THINKABOUT 20 - THE SIX STEPS

- Read, mark, learn and inwardly digest this chapter: this WILL happen to you
- Share and discuss it with colleagues
- Practice the six steps, so you are ready to use them when the issue arises

WHY YOU SHOULD LOVE COMPLAINTS

A friend told me about a meal out they had had that wasn't very good. So, I asked: "Did you complain?" And, you've guessed it, you're a step ahead of me, they answered: "No, if you complain they don't seem to like it. So, I just won't bother going there again."

And how common is this story?

- The customer loses eventually because they will have less choice of places to eat. They will often revert to safer options like branded restaurants or supermarkets
- The restaurant will lose because their reputation and organization will suffer and they won't have a clue why this has happened
- The community will lose because this organization will struggle at best and go out of business at worst

All because they weren't bright enough to understand that they should love complaints. Complaints are an insight into what needs to be changed or developed in order to build customer amazement and customer loyalty. Whether you think they are justified or not, reasonable or unreasonable, they are giving feedback that you desperately need in order to build and grow your organization in the hyper competitive world of the empowered consumer.

So, the old fear of complaints must be banished in favour of welcoming complaints. Then, and only then, no matter how good you are, will you continue to thrive and grow.

A simple rule would be to change the word "complaint" to "compliment". Because that's exactly what they are. Your customer is telling you that they care enough about you to feedback on what they would like to see changed in order to be able to carry on using you in the future and, what is more, to recommend you to all their friends.

Get a Grip on Your Ego and Welcome Complaints.

THINKABOUT 21 - COMPLAINTS SYSTEMS

- Make sure you have GREAT complaint management systems that not only follow the four principles but also, of course, don't aim to merely 'manage' complaints but are designed to actively turn them into triumphs for both parties
- Don't be a wet flannel: have a blow their socks off system – this is a HUGE opportunity

PART FOUR

HOW TO GET REFERRALS

REFERRAL SYSTEMS, MAKE IT EASY BY THE INCH

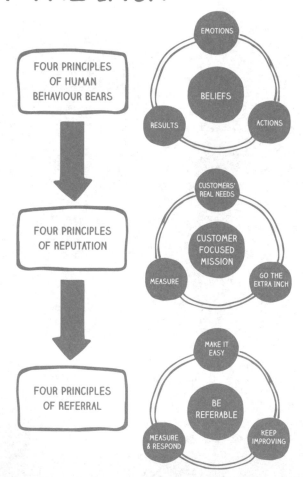

FOUR PRINCIPLES OF HUMAN BEHAVIOUR BEARS

EMOTIONS
BELIEFS
RESULTS
ACTIONS

FOUR PRINCIPLES OF REPUTATION

CUSTOMERS' REAL NEEDS
CUSTOMER FOCUSED MISSION
MEASURE
GO THE EXTRA INCH

FOUR PRINCIPLES OF REFERRAL

MAKE IT EASY
BE REFERABLE
MEASURE & RESPOND
KEEP IMPROVING

Referral systems don't need to be overly complicated. In fact, the more complicated you make something, the less likely it is that people will use it. In a nutshell, simple, easy systems get great results.

Examples:

* One-click ordering
* Regular simple payment schemes
* The poker chip system

Which brings us on to the first point, 'Why People Don't Bother to Refer an Organization'

* So many companies fall into the trap of asking the standard 'How likely is it that you would recommend us to a friend,' question without any follow up. That's a question. It's not a call to action. It has little real output
* Companies don't develop a system that makes it easy for customers to refer them. And if it's not easy they're not going to refer you. They are too busy, distracted, uninterested etc. – life is busy enough already!

There are five things that you have to consider for great referral systems:

1. Get referrals from the right people
2. Get referrals to the right people
3. Get referrals for the right reasons
4. At the right time
5. In the right way

All these steps should be taken slowly and done inch by inch (to make it easy for them) – don't go for it like a bull in a china shop!

THINKABOUT 22: REFERRAL SYSTEMS

- Use the information provided so far to produce a simple referral system that you can continually and systematically use
- Draw a flow chart, inch by inch, to allow for all different scenarios (depending on how the customer reacts or what type of referrals/leads you want to generate
- Implement it inch by inch
- Evaluate and evolve it inch by inch with continual feedback gathering and regular systematic reviews

ACTIVE OR PASSIVE?

- Active referrals are systems that involve actively following up
- Passive systems don't involve actively follow up. They rely on your customer doing all the work

Of course, active systems are generally harder to make work but they are much more effective when they do work. They are also much more suited to relationship and partnership situations, they can be better described as a sniper approach.

Passive systems are easier to put in place but very often have low success rates due to lack of customer motivation. They are more of a shotgun approach and are more suited to transactional, lower value emotional situations.

Whatever is most suitable for your organization and market, the following principles and steps apply in the same way. You just need to adapt them to your situation, without losing the processes and principles embedded in them.

HERE'S HOW YOU DO IT:

1. FROM THE RIGHT PEOPLE

The right people are the ones who love you and have given you permission. They are the ones who told you they thought you were great in your feedback systems. Do not ask for **referrals from anyone else.** If you do, then you're a blithering idiot.

- If you ask someone who rated you as 'poor' or 'satisfactory' for a referral, you are essentially telling them that you don't care about their feedback
- And if you ask for referrals without asking for feedback first, you're essentially saying that you don't care about what customers think, you just want to sell more of your stuff. Who would want to recommend or refer an organization like this? But, this tends to be the default situation for most referral systems – another reason why most referral systems don't work

Remember to go through this process with an inch-by-inch approach. Always start by getting permission to speak with them. Never get greedy.

2. TO THE RIGHT PEOPLE

The right people are those who fit the profile of your ideal customer. If you don't have a profile for your ideal customer, then you need to create one. Don't target just anyone!

Creating the profile for your ideal customer starts by answering questions like these:

	Business-to-Business (B2B)	Business-to-Consumer (B2C)
What is their role in their job?	X	
What is their level of responsibility?	X	
Where do they live?		X
How old are they?		X
Are they a specific gender?		X
What industry are they in?	X	X
How might they be struggling?	X	X
What do they need help with?	X	X
Who might they naturally be turning to?	X	X
What type of marketing do they mostly do?	X	
How could you genuinely help them?	X	X
How do they assess new suppliers?	X	X

By the time you are done creating a profile for the ideal customer, it should be so clear that you can envision this person as if he/she were standing in front of you.

So now you can tell your existing customers exactly what type of customer they could refer you to, otherwise they won't know.

- Use the questions above to form a profile of your ideal customer
- Check, balance and hone it continually

3. FOR THE RIGHT REASONS

Why do you want to get referrals?

This all comes back to your customer focused mission. Getting referrals helps you keep your marketing costs down so that you can also keep your prices reasonable. It also helps you continually keep on your toes and improve your organization processes to continually create more value for your existing customers.

Any other reason is you just wanting to sell more of your stuff – thus making you remarkably unreferable!

Why would these people want to refer you?

- You've provided them with great service
- You've gathered feedback excellently
- You've made it easy for them to refer you
- You've done small things that are easy to say "yes" to

What's in it for them to refer you?

When people refer you to others they are putting their own reputation on the line, and going out of their way for no direct reward. So, make sure that everything you do is designed in a way that makes them look really good when they refer you. You can't ever let them down. You must have earned their trust enough so that you are seen as someone who is genuinely worth referring.

You must be systematically highly referable, this is non-negotiable. A referral is an emotional act, you need to have a strong emotional tie with your customer to incentivise them to do this beautiful act for you.

Any other reason is short lived, fatuous, counterproductive and contradictory. For example: offering incentives or free prize draws!

How do you spread a reputation of being someone worth referring?

- When someone refers you, you then need to blow the socks off of both parties

Party 1: The 'Referee'
The person being referred to you should get a better deal than if they had found you through normal processes. You reward them for being referred.

Why?

- Because your existing customer put their reputation on the line for you – you need to support their faith
- Because it's much more cost effective to find people this way. That means you should be able to give them a better deal. Think of all that marketing time, money and effort you've saved

Party 2: The 'Referrer'

Make sure that you have a great thank-you system for all referrers. This could be a simple phone call. It could be offering to do a little work for them free of charge, it could be a bunch of flowers, it could be special gift or event. The important thing is a thank-you, not a bribe. You **never** advertise it in advance; you just do it – as you would do with a great friend, because they are being a great friend to you. This is very important.

You have to make sure that whatever you do to say thank-you is going to make the organization glad that it helped refer you. If you get this right then they will continue to refer your services. Not only will you have received a referral from them, you will also have put them into the habit of referring you! It's amazing that when someone refers you once, they are much more open to referring you on a regular basis.

THINKABOUT 24 - REFERRAL FOLLOW UP SYSTEMS

* Create 'blow your socks off' offers and systems for referees
* Create 'blow your socks off' thank-you systems for referrers
* Gather feedback and continually hone these systems

4. AT THE RIGHT TIME

The right time to ask for referrals is directly after receiving feedback. This is included in the feedback system we discussed earlier.

But don't rush it. Wait until they say they're happy and willing, never before!

5. IN THE RIGHT WAY

- Always gather feedback first!
- Do it inch by inch. Ask for one referral at a time
- Make it fun. Don't be boring. This whole system is about building a relationship. And don't sound like you're reading from a script
- Explain why you're asking for referrals:

1st inch

"Would you mind us asking a question that would be helpful to our organization?"

Yes/No

Next Inch

"We aim to grow mainly through personal referrals. It helps us keep costs down and focus on doing as well as we can for existing customers. If we asked you for a referral would you be willing to consider helping us?"

Yes/No

Next Inch

"If we call you in a week about this, would that be okay?"

Ask permission to get referred. Remember that "no" is okay.

✓ Always follow up on your promises. If you say that you're going to call back in a week, be sure that you make that phone call
✓ Make sure you thank them for referring you

6. DO IT!

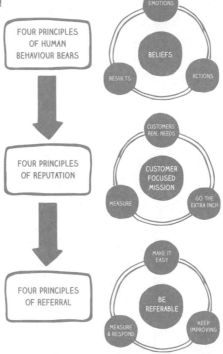

FOUR PRINCIPLES OF HUMAN BEHAVIOUR BEARS

EMOTIONS
BELIEFS
RESULTS
ACTIONS

FOUR PRINCIPLES OF REPUTATION

CUSTOMERS' REAL NEEDS
CUSTOMER FOCUSED MISSION
MEASURE
GO THE EXTRA INCH

FOUR PRINCIPLES OF REFERRAL

MAKE IT EASY
BE REFERABLE
MEASURE & RESPOND
KEEP IMPROVING

THINKABOUT 25 - DOING IT

- Think it through using our guidance
- Ask key loyal customers for their opinion on your system and wording
- Test it inch by inch
- Roll it out as it starts working
- Never go too quickly: if you let anyone down at this stage, you're going to mess both relationships up!

7. FEEDBACK AND THANKS

Go the extra inch.

✓ Keep the referee informed about progress
✓ Implement your thank-you system quickly and generously. If it's a genuine referral, even if you don't get any business from it, you should say thank-you with your systems. It shows that, whatever happens, you're genuine and very referable
✓ Consider having a continual small reward system for customers who refer you, if you have systems that can cope professionally with this

8. FOLLOW UP

Go the extra inch. Thank them again later down the road.

What if you were to call them three months from the time you got the referral and say, "I just wanted to let you know that we've done some really good business with the person you referred us to – thank-you again for referring us."

THINKABOUT 26 - GREAT THANKS AND FOLLOW UP SYSTEMS

- Look for great systems every day as a customer
- Search the web and customer experience blogs for more examples
- Create and hone your system continually: it can NEVER be too good!

Great Examples:

Let's take a moment to look at a few great passive referral systems (they help understand the ideas and we have already run through the 'active' referral process step by step).

_____

My wife got an envelope in a delivered vegetable box that read "Things in Threes are the Bees Knees."

Without even opening the envelope, we can already see that it's fun. Of course, we would want to open it. When we opened the envelope, the note inside reads as follows:

"Give the Gift of Adventure to Three Lucky People"

We've been hooked by the cover and now the message is pulling us in. All that's left is to give a call to action.

It clearly explains exactly what they want you to do in a very easy-to-follow format. It reads as follows:

1. Open the envelope.

2. Write your account number on the voucher. You can find your account number on your receipt.

3. Give the vouchers to your favourite people so they can try one of our organic fruit and vegetable boxes.

Wow! That voucher does everything quite wonderfully. It's fun and makes it very easy on the customer to refer three of their friends.

Each voucher then explains to the referee exactly what they need to do in order to claim their free fruit and vegetable box.

This passive referral system is absolutely perfect.

Another card from a competitor of the previous example. That wasn't as much of a fun read...

"Veg for your friends. £10 for you. Free cookbook for them."

It's not as 'in your face' as the previous example but it's still a good card. Again, the process is very simple. The card has small tokens that you simply tear off and give to a friend.

This example demonstrates that a feedback and referral system should be fun, creative, and provide a direct, yet simple call to action. Whatever you do, make sure that your system is:

* Open
* Transparent
* Engaging
* Clear
* Simple

Note: the above systems are all to be used in transactional and emotional organizations. If you're in a different style of business use the principles to design a system that works brilliantly for you.

REPETITION AND REINFORCEMENT

Now we've outlined the principles and steps for effective referral systems, it's time for a little bit of repetition and enforcement:

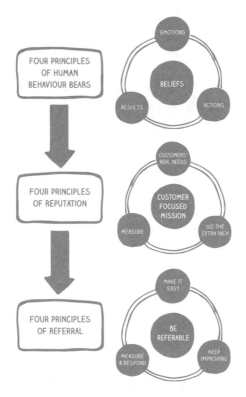

Everyone bangs on about 'getting referrals'. But they conveniently forget the one crucial point that no one wants to give you referrals. They're too busy getting on with their own life!

Don't get caught in the much promoted trap of thinking streams of referrals will follow a positive answer to the question, 'How likely is it that you would refer us?' That's just a starting point!

But, referrals are by far the most powerful and profitable way of building a organization. So, how do we get them, and what can we do to make it actually work?

Let's look at it from the individual customer's point of view:

Whether or not we liked the customer experience isn't what motivates us to take the risky step of referring something (or someone). We have all the following issues to sort out first:

- Do I want to be responsible if my friend has a bad experience?
- Does this provider give the impression of being able to cope effectively with extra custom?
- Will the provider be upset with me if this goes wrong or doesn't happen?
- How does it make me look? How does it affect my professional and personal standing?
- How easy is this organization's offer to explain to someone else?
- Does it look like I'm getting some sort of kickback or special treatment in exchange? How does this affect my own reputation?

The key is this: and the order of this is CRUCIAL: get it wrong, and in today's market, you'll really screw up!

i. Be genuinely referable first
ii. Make it easy
iii. Proactive systems
iv. Great responses to all feedback
v. Elastic & Velcro Marketing systems
vi. Right process
vii. Easy and engaging processes
viii. Keep honing and improving
ix. Measure & respond

That's how to get referrals!

THINKABOUT 27 - WHY MOST PEOPLE WON'T BOTHER TO REFER YOU

- Teach the above ideas to others

HOW TO
FOLLOW UP
REFERRALS

Many people believe that cold referrals can be hard to follow up. Here's some help in this area.

The main factor that you have to keep in the back of your mind when dealing with cold referrals is that they do not trust you. With so many people bombarding them with offers, can you really blame them for not trusting you? They don't even know you! For all they know, you're just another annoyance trying to take their money.

You have to be remarkable to get past their understandable barriers! Again, average just doesn't cut it.

The good news is that you already have a system in place that is designed to build your reputation, so are you ready to get started?

Let's be honest. No one wants to speak with you. Everyone's too busy. Therefore, you have to make sure that you're worth talking to. You only have a few seconds to grab their attention so make sure that you get the idea across in that time. Focus on their real needs.

AN EASY INCH-BY-INCH APPROACH

Here's a step-by-step approach to help you with cold referrals. This is designed for a B2B situation, but you will see that they can be easily adapted to suit any customer relationship. Remember to approach this process in the same way that you do your other calls. Always ask for permission and utilise the inch-by-inch approach.

Step 1: Introduction
Start off a call by giving the customer your name and the reason for your call. Time is a valuable resource: give them a great reason to spend this valuable resource on you. Always be honest!

Tell them the results you achieved for the referrer. Those results were rated as 'great' (otherwise you would not have asked for a referral) so now you have a chance to brag a little bit about it. The referrer would be happy to confirm everything you tell them.

Next is an area where a lot of people really drop the ball. You are not going to be able to help everyone – you have to be honest. Tell them that there might be a way that you can help them get similar results. Don't say that you can definitely help them. How could you possibly know with 100% certainty that you can help them? You don't even know them.

Ask whether this is a good time or if they would prefer that you call them later. You need permission to continue. If it's not a good time, then ask if you can call back at a better time.

You're only going to have a few seconds to earn enough trust to be given permission to continue with the call. Make sure that you craft an introduction that includes everything we mentioned above. This introduction should be between two to three sentences. If you are given permission to continue, then do so. If not, then either reschedule the call or end it. Never try to pitch to anyone who is not interested.

Step 2: Explain Why You Called Them
This one is going to be a value statement based on your customer focused mission. Just be honest and explain exactly what it is that you have to offer.

Make sure you also use this sort of phrase, "our typical customers are those who have a limited budget and want to get excellent results without having to spend a fortune."

Step 3: Get Permission to Ask a Genuine Question
You have gone through the introduction and explained what it is that you have to offer. You have their full attention at this point you're going to start peeling the onion.

Lead off with this question:
"Does this seem at all like a product/service that might be of interest to you?"

Listen to their response closely. When they are finished, then you ask another question. Regardless of their answer being "yes" or "no," respond with this:

"Okay. Can I ask you one question?"

Asking for permission again builds trust and makes them comfortable. It's much better to ask for permission than it is to instantly try selling them something.

Step 4: The Question
The next question depends on their answer to, "can I ask you one question?"

If they answer yes, ask: "Can I ask what your main issues/opportunities/wants/desires/pains/problems/needs in this area are and how you solve them at the moment?"

If they answer no, ask: "If I called you back at a better time would you be willing to discuss your main issues or needs in this area, and how you solve them at the moment?"

The trick is to really listen to them, peel the onion gently with open questions. If they tell you "no," then thank them and end the call. It's perfectly okay for them to say no.

Step 5: Get to the Point
By now you will have built up quite a bit of trust. You should also know the problems that they are facing. It's time to get to the point. Work deeply with the customer's real needs. Peel the onion some more.

Here's what you could say:

"I don't want to waste your time and I don't really know yet whether our services might be useful to you. Do you mind if I ask two more questions to determine if it's worth scheduling a more in-depth conversation?"

If they answer "no" then thank them for their time, peel the onion to find out more information if you can – what WOULD they want to talk with you about, now or later – and at the right time, thank them and end the call.

If they answer "yes" then move on to the next step.

Step 6: Ask the Two Questions
Here are the two questions that you ask. Again, make sure that you listen carefully to their response.

"Who are your customers and why do they buy from you as opposed to your competitors?"

This question establishes their current situation.

"What would be the main things you'd like to do better, and what concerns might you have about taking on a new supplier?"

This opens the door as to what they want to know about you.

Step 7: Ending the Call
The end of the call is a very important process that is often overlooked. This is your opportunity to make their life easier, show them attention and build further trust.

Three things must happen at the end of the call.

1. Confirm everything that has been discussed. Then decide what's going to happen next. You can schedule a more in-depth call or even a personal visit. On the other hand, your organization might not be a good fit with theirs. In that case, you absolutely must not try to "make it work." Don't bc afraid to say "no."

2. Provide even more value to them by telling them about (genuine) extras that you are able to offer them because they were referred.

3. Genuinely thank them before ending the call. Your goal is to reassure them that they have made a good decision, whatever it is.

Then take it from there with your normal sales processes.

THINKABOUT 28 - 'COLD' REFERRALS

- Adapt the above information to suit your situation
- Be guided by the 'Customer's REAL Needs' principle
- Learn and teach the wording and principles
- Continually listen, measure, hone and refine

OVERCOMING 'OBJECTIONS'

That one word 'objection' can seem scary. Well we have some good news for you. The word 'objections' is absolute rubbish. There's no such thing in the business world.

Statements that are seen as objections are, in fact, just genuine concerns from the potential customer for good reasons – primarily about how they can get the best result for themselves.

You would do exactly the same thing if you were in their shoes!

There are concerns that are important, and the action to take is listen, peel and address these legitimate concerns. Whether or not you get a sale is not really important right now. These concerns are paramount.

This is NOT a battle!

Remember your customer focused mission and the customer's real needs. Everything you do should be based on listening and welcoming these concerns. This is the only way that you will ever know how you can genuinely help a customer and build a great long-term relationship so they can in turn refer their contacts to you over time or not.

Remember that no is OK, if you get the relationship right they may want to do business with you later, and refer others to you. Either way, you've not compromised your status of being genuinely remarkable. You've not compromised yourself just to get the sale.

It also reveals the most efficient way to help them.

- Listen deeply. It always seems to come back to listening, doesn't it? That's because so few companies truly listen to their customers. The ones that do are successful
- Peel the onion with open questions. Make sure that they give you permission to do this
- Determine their needs and 'desired results'. It's never about what you want. It's about what they want
- Only try to solve a problem when they ask you to. Never try solving their problems without permission
- Work together to find a win/win solution, either you can do business together for the right reasons, or you can't do business together for the right reasons. Never try and do either for the wrong reasons

And then you'll be fine.

THINKABOUT 29 - CUSTOMER CONCERNS (NOT 'OBJECTIONS')

- Adapt the above information to suit your situation
- Be guided by the key principles in everything
- Learn and teach the principle: we only want a sale or no sale for the RIGHT reasons, never either for the WRONG reasons
- Continually listen, measure, hone and refine

KEEP REPEATING
AND IMPROVING

Once you have developed a system to use with your customers, you can start focusing on other sources of referrals, as already mentioned. Many people tend to overlook them.

Keep following the same four principles and you will eventually be able to start asking for referrals.

* Get your mission right
* Think of your customers' real needs first
* Build the relationship
* Put measures in place to keep improving

If you don't continuously improve your system then your competition will catch up with you. When you get it right, someone else is going to notice – and the more successful you are, the harder your competitors will fight to lure away your suc

PART FIVE

SYSTEM OVERVIEW AND ACTION PLAN

SYSTEM OVERVIEW IN 10 STEPS

1. It's all up to you. You're in charge of what you do. How much do you really want to get this right?

2. It's a marathon not a sprint. Take it slowly and get it right.

3. You can't get reliable reputation and referrals until you're reliably remarkable and referable.

4. In the SR world of two-way mass communication and online transparency there are no shortcuts and no places to hide in the long run.

5. Build your remarkability and referability slowly and steadily using the four 'Great or Poor' principles.

6. Feedback first. Great feedback systems power great organizations.

7. Build win/win responses to all levels of feedback.

8. Customers will only refer you if you make it easy and engaging and they trust your competence.

9. Take small steps in everything you do, test, measure and develop.

10. Continually keep improving.

THE REFERRALS FORMULA: FIVE STEPS TO ACTUALLY DO IT

THE REFERRAL FORMULA

Mindset: We want to be 'referrable'

Knowledge: Continual feedback and research: what's the market and what do customers think and want?

Systems: Customer Focused Mission, Customer's REAL Needs Filter, Go the Extra Inch, Measure

Action: Be 'referrable' Gather feedback, Engage, Build loyalty

Action: Create partnership and keep improving

ACTION PLAN: EIGHT STEPS TO SUCCESS USING THIS BOOK

Knowledge without action is delusion. Action without knowledge is reckless. You now have the knowledge, so you're now ready for action.

Suggested Action Plan:

1. Read the book in full (done!)

2. Go back and mark/highlight/note key areas of interest and opportunity for your situation.

3. Write out and print out:
    a. The 10 steps
    b. The 'Referral Formula' diagram
    c. The four principles
    The act of writing them out will help you learn them.

4. Share and teach what you have learned to those you need to help you do this.

5. Set up a structured weekly 'Go the Extra Inch' process with the aim of working on and improving one thing per week. Use the exercises in each of the sections to guide you.

6. Work on one process at a time, filter it through the customers' real needs.

7. Never stop. Success is a journey, not a destination.

8. Get a professional coach/helper as needed. This is too important to not get right, and far too costly to get wrong!

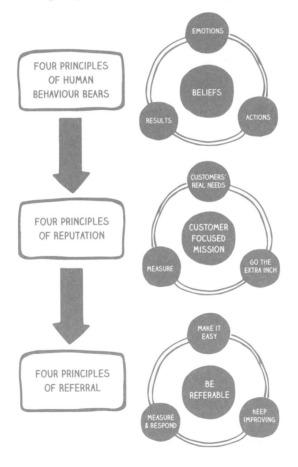

THANK YOU

Thank you, sincerely, for taking the time and effort to buy and read this book. The best of luck with your journey, and one last thing – 'no farmer ever ploughed his field by turning it over in his mind' – the key is action. Small steps. Do it! We aim to practice what we preach:

- If you've found the book helpful, please share this news with your friends and colleagues
- If you haven't, please let us know why, and we will improve the next edition

ABOUT THE AUTHORS

Guy Arnold is the founder and Managing Director of 'Sales through Service' and 'Investors in Feedback'. He coaches, trains and accredits customer experience, loyalty, reputation and referral systems for organisations of all types and sizes. He is the author of three books on the subject of Customer Experience Systems that produce continual and consistent repeat sales, cross sales, up sales and referrals. Before this he was a turnaround expert and brand builder in the licensed and leisure industry in the UK, and a Director of a FTSE 100 Company.

Russell Wood is a professional trainer and business advisor. He has held senior board, commercial and operational roles in the gaming and leisure industry. He works with pub, leisure and local authority clients providing training, management of client contracts, and developing gaming and re-tail operations. A former Fellow of The British Institute of Inn-keeping, he has held gaming licences in the UK and the Isle of Man; represented the BBPA in government consultations; is an associate member of BACTA and a UK Personal Licence holder.

We offer advice, training and coaching in all subjects concerning improving your R&R. Please contact us to find out more:
support@salesthroughservice.com